In a city of seven million lonely souls...

...There are *hundreds* of businesses dedicated to bringing people *together*.

Roses

I'm lookin' for *Meserov?*

13th floor, lady.

Elevators are over there.

There is only *one* to tear them *apart*.

Mine.
Welcome to *Heartbreak Incorporated.*
Please.
Take a seat.

I'm Sherri Rubenstein.
My *lawyer* referred me?
mmh
My husband's *Ian Rubenstein.*
The *nightclub owner?*
And he's taken up with *another girl.*
How do you know?
If it were a *boy,* you wouldn't be as mad.
I want her GONE.

She's **uglier** than me!
I do **everything** I'm supposed to.
This is **Halston**.
My hair? Is **Alexandre**.
I never talk about myself.
I take **bupkis**.
It's all about **him**.
And he's going around the club behind my back with this ugly bitch!
Maybe you **should** be more selfish.
Nobody appreciates what they get **for free**.
He's **all I have**.
And she's bleeding him **dry**.

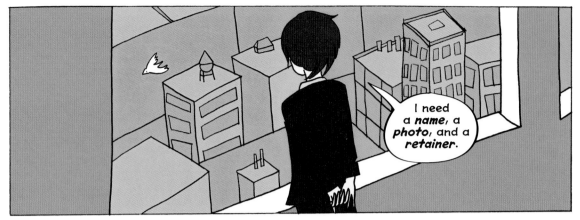

I need a *name*, a *photo*, and a *retainer*.

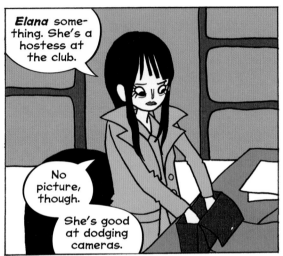

Elana something. She's a hostess at the club.

No picture, though.

She's good at dodging cameras.

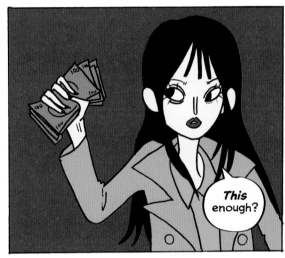

This enough?

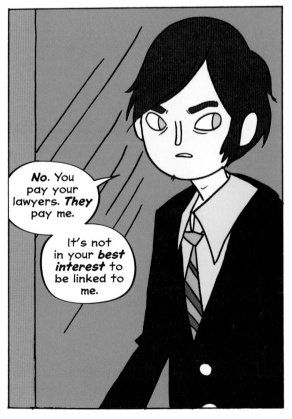

No. You pay your lawyers. *They* pay me.

It's not in your *best interest* to be linked to me.

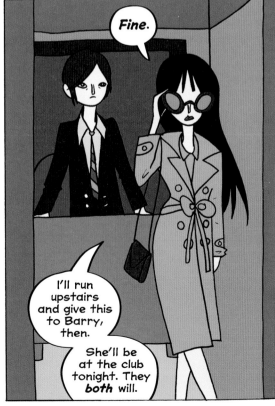

Fine.

I'll run upstairs and give this to Barry, then.

She'll be at the club tonight. They *both* will.

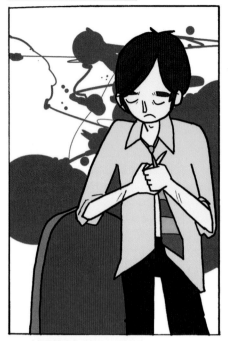

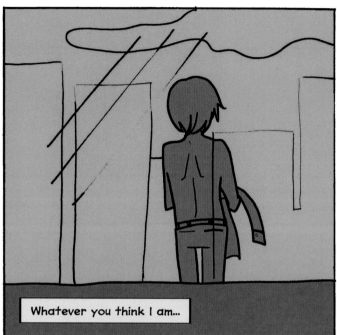

Whatever you think I am...

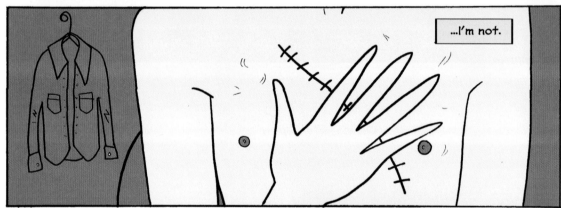

...I'm not.

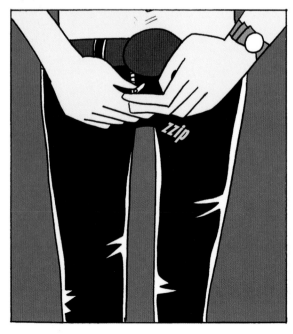

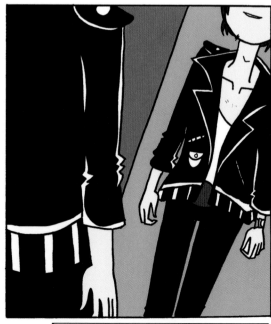

But whatever you want me to be?

I can become it.
DON'T WALK
They say Mick usually shows up on Thursdays--
Don't ook no is th Ig
This line isn't even moving. We'l never get in--
No! I want to stay.
Hey, it Ultra Violet
Your desires...
...You wear them so nakedly upon your faces.
Once upon a time, I did too.

aaaaaaah

freak out!

Ian, I wanted to introduce you to my friend Bianca.
Ian! Marty sends his love and respect.

freak out!

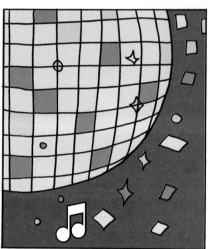

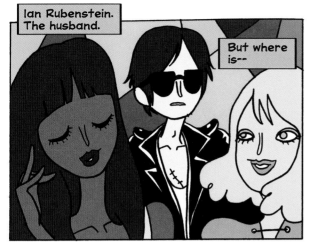

Ian Rubenstein.
The husband.

But where is--

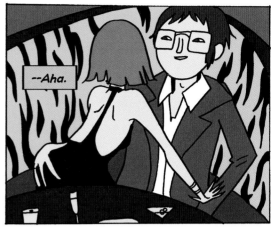

--Aha.

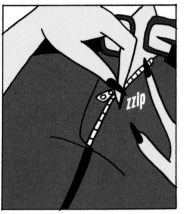

zzip

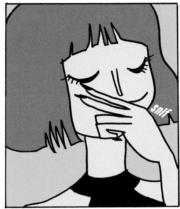

snif

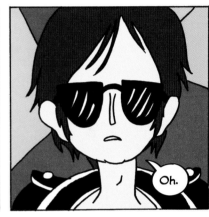

Oh.

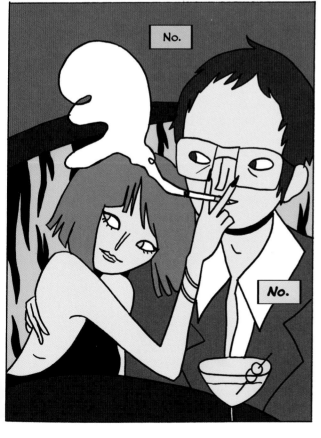

No.

No.

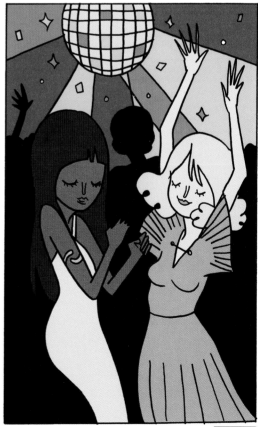

NO.

RING!
RING!
RING!
mmf
mnuh?
It's me.
TELEPHONE
FFT
There's been a *complication*.

Sherri, why do you want him back?
Love?
Inertia?
Spite?
Be ***honest***.
Because he's going to die.
He's going to sign over the club to her, and then he's going to have a heart attack.
How do you know this?
I know ***her***.

Or, I did.

el
DORADO
EL
DORADO

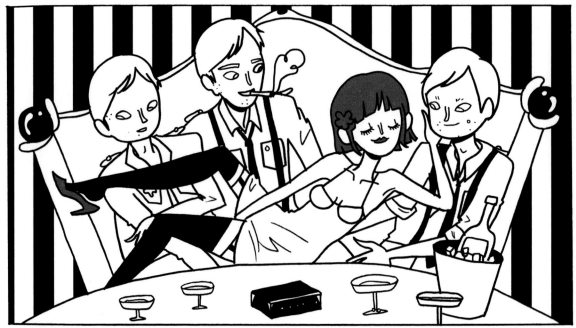

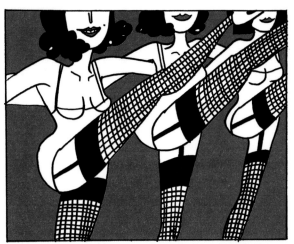

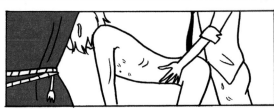

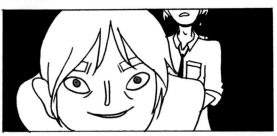

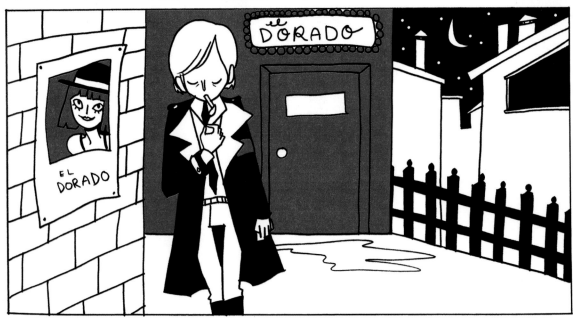

It was in ***Berlin.***

Just a minute, *lieblings*.
How **long**, Mackie?
A week, maybe, before his heart gives out.
Greedy boy.
I was hungry.

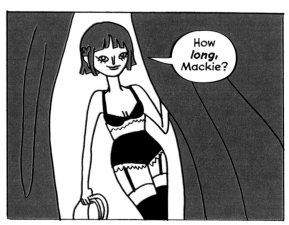

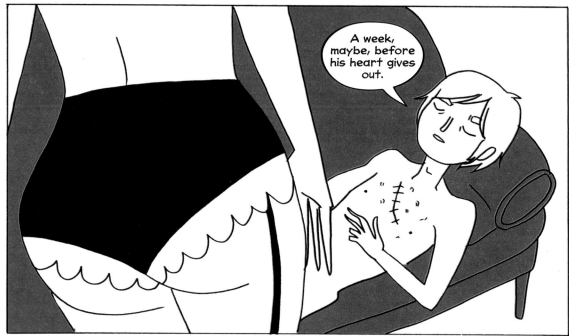

We're **two of a kind**, you could say.
Then **do your job** and get **rid** of her.
I've **faked** orgasms for that man for **too goddamn long** for her to come and take all this away from me.
I earned it. It's **mine**.
I understand.

I doubt it.
We all do what we must, to survive.
It'll be done by morning.
Unless I *lose*.
Do you lose very often, Misha?
Hardly ever.

I went back to the club.

Yes, Sir
i can boogie
The night, as they say, was still young.
And I was hungry.
A year from her.
Six months from him.

Little pieces of lives

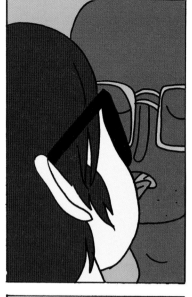

to sustain a beast

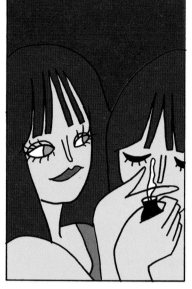

without a heart.

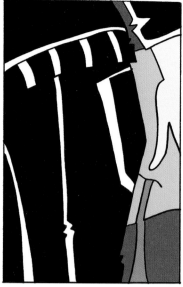

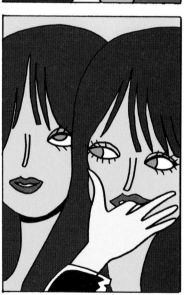

Incubare: to lie upon.

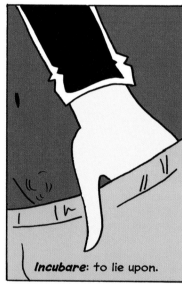

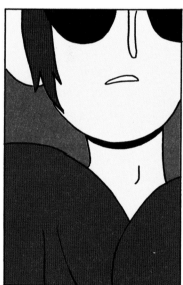

Succubare: to lie beneath.

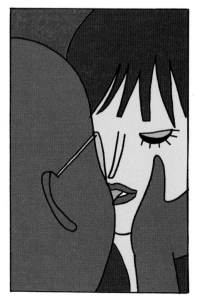

So deceptively specific.

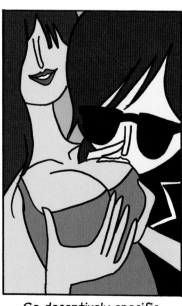

What if one likes to *switch*?

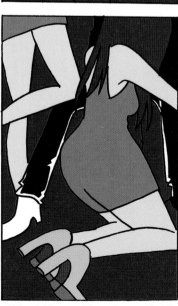

You. Go.
tap
Mackie.
Still so pretty.
It's Misha, now.
Ah. Back to your roots.
This is my town, Esther.
My territory.
You need to leave.

HA
HA HA
HA
HAHA
HA
HA
No.
I'm not done here yet.
Join me.
We used to be good together.
Elena, c'mere!
Andy wants to take your photo.

I **can't**, Ian baby.
I just ran into the **oldest** friend, and he has **gossip**.
You're going to kill him.
Of course.
It's what we **do**.
Not **me**.
Not anymore.
Mackie, you **child**.
--!

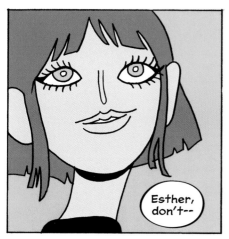

Esther, don't--

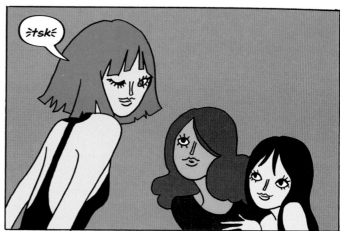

>tsk<

All your little *rules*, Mackie.

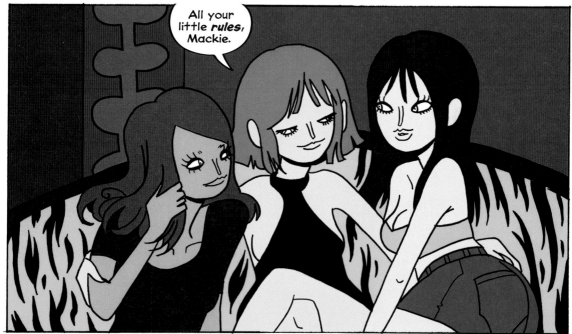

Don't feed all the way.

Don't enchant them.

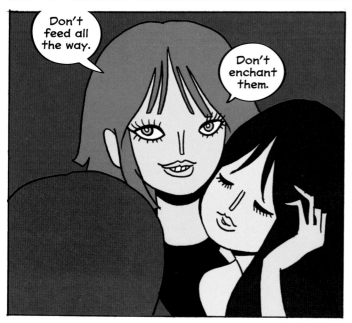

Esther, *stop it.*

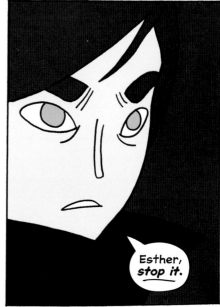

None of it matters.
You're still a ***parasite***.

One of these days you'll get over yourself and ***enjoy*** it.

Come *home*, Misha.
You don't have to be so lonely.
No.
You struggle so hard, and yet to what result?
Is the *world* better for it?
Are *you?*
...No.
Ian is *not* a good man.
And we are no judges.
Who cares? He will die happy.

We persuaded ourselves we were doing good, killing those soldiers.
I wonder if we were just soaking their cruelty into ourselves.
That would be the final irony, wouldn't it?
Trying to take only the evil ones, and in doing so, becoming irrevocably tainted by them.
We are what we eat.
Yeah.

I guess we are.

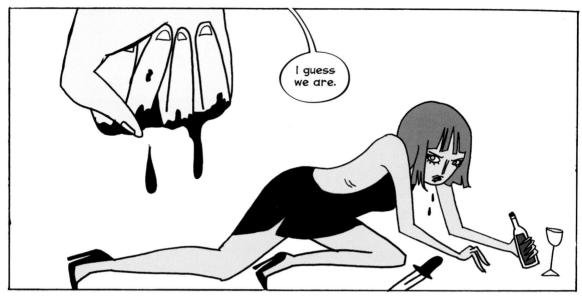

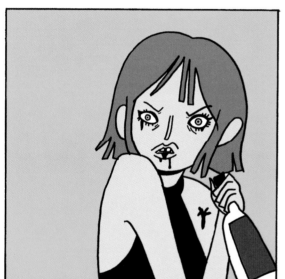

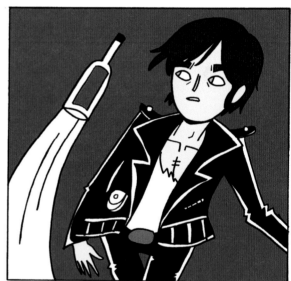

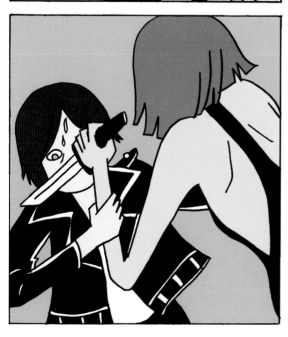

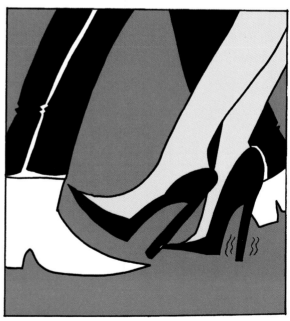

There's only one way to kill us.

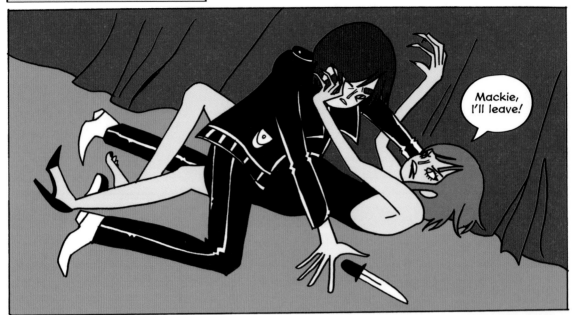

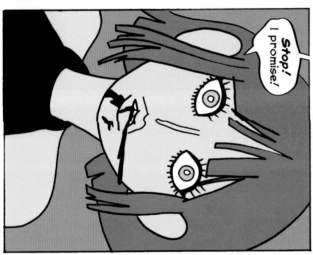

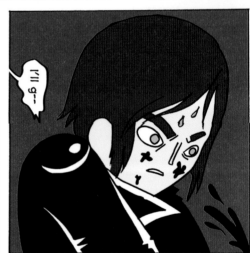

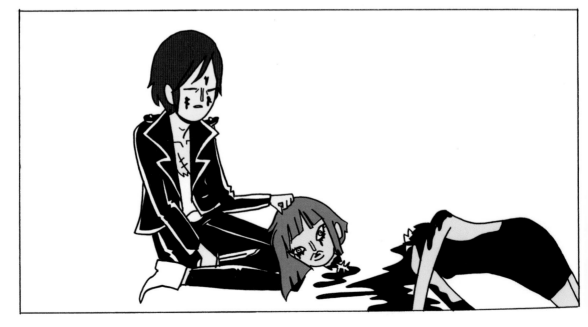

FOOM
shhf
fft

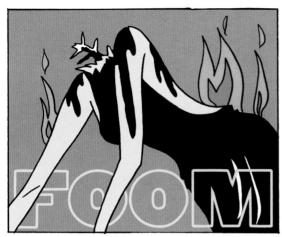

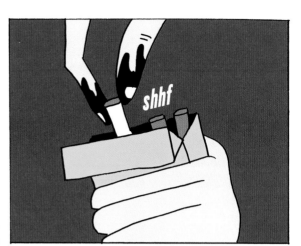

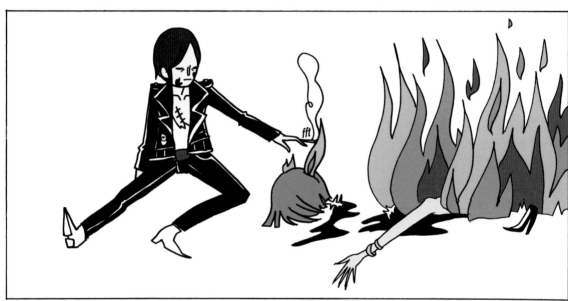

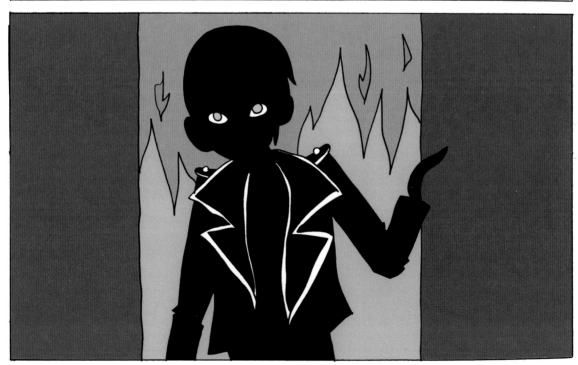

WEEEOOO
WEEEOOO
WEEEOOO
NYC 503
It is done.
She's gone?
Yeah. Ian's ***all yours*** again.
That is, until the ***next*** one.

THE END.

Fig. 37.

H
I
I
G
K
E
L
C
F
D
A
B

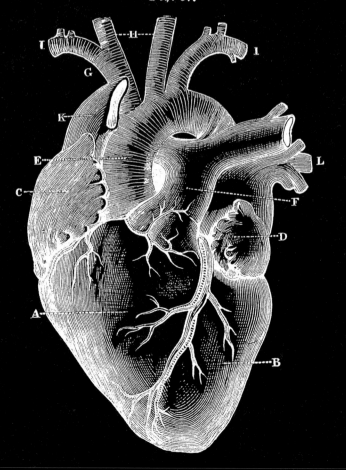

Leather & Lace

by Magen Cubed

There were three kinds of teeth in the world. Dorian Villeneuve had seen only two before the night in the woods outside Devereux city limits: the kind for biting, and the kind for tearing. Vampires, werewolves, all manner of shifter: they were creatures with sharp animal teeth and a taste for blood. Dorian had a set of fangs of his own, after all, and he knew plenty about blood. The third kind of teeth he never saw on a hunt before: big, flat, and made for grinding bones. These were the teeth of man-eaters.

It wasn't until Dorian watched a set sink into his bicep that he took the expression to heart.

The thing about man-eaters was that there were so *few* of them. Things with fangs liked to feed on humans, take a drink or a bite here and there. But they hardly ever killed. The only thing that came out of the dark to eat men whole were wendigos, and wendigos were nearly extinct. The few that existed kept a low profile and minded their manners. So for five bodies to turn up in as many weeks, gored by antlers and gnawed on by grinding teeth? It was the strangest turn that their strange county had seen in many a year.

However, at that moment Dorian was less concerned with the surpassing rarity of wendigos than the fact that one was trying to chew his arm off. He hauled back his good arm with all his greater-than-human strength, and punched the wendigo between its glassy black eyes. The wendigo snarled, dropping Dorian in the dirt. The wendigo was a great, shaggy beast with a stag's head atop a well-muscled frame. Upright, the beast pushed seven feet tall, and that's not including the antlers. Those antlers sprouted from its head in a crown of bones and sharp points. Those flat, crushing teeth gnashed, chewing on the warm breath streaming from its blood-soaked jaw and flared nostrils.

With a snarl, a hooved foot came up, ready to stomp Dorian. It was an anticlimactic way to go, even by his standards.

"You may wanna move."

A shot rang out like a clap of thunder between the trees. The wendigo reared back and bellowed in pain. Another blast put him down in a heap of muscle and gnarled antlers. Two bullets tore through his back, the hair singed by gunpowder. Dorian scurried out of the way, dragging his chewed arm with him. When he looked up, Cash Leroy stood where the wendigo had just towered over him.

Cash, with his sawed-off shotgun and punch-black eye, offering Dorian a hand and a smirk. Dorian took the hand, but couldn't muster a smile in return.

"Show-off," he grumbled.

"I told you not to run out ahead of me." Cash tucked the sawed-off under his arm to examine the bite in Dorian's. "Bambi took a chomp out of you, didn't he?"

"I didn't want to let him get away," Dorian protested with a wince. "He was moving too fast for you to keep up."

"And you call *me* the show-off."

Cash's callused fingers gently traced over the teeth marks. The bites were bloody, but shallow. It wouldn't take long to heal. This close, with his light touch, Cash smelled of sweat and his favorite woodsy aftershave. Dorian's heart thudded against his ribs, but from excitement rather than pain. He swallowed as Cash's sleepy eyes, one purpled from the wendigo's fist, darted up to meet his.

"I still shouldn't have left you out here." The smile returned, small and sheepish as it was. "Better get you to back to the car, get you fixed up. Have to haul this carcass back to Fritz."

Reminded of the dead wendigo, Dorian's heartrate quickly fell. "And if you expect me to drag this thing around with a bum arm, you're mistaken."

Cash's smile broke into a chuckle. "Yessir."

* * *

"That, my friends, is a wendigo."

Detective Hayden Fritz peered through his wireframe glasses at the shaggy corpse of the stag-man hybrid. The body was laid out on the gurney, hauled from the back of Cash's pick-up truck for delivery behind the 23rd Precinct. Fritz's bifocals blew his eyes wide as he pulled the length out of his tape measure.

"That was my thought." Cash mumbled, leaning against the driver's-side door of his truck. His hands warmed themselves in his jacket pockets, and when he spoke again, his cigarette shifted between pursed lips. "Don't recall the last time I saw one."

"Me, neither," Fritz paused to answer. Muttering under his breath, he took measurements of the wendigo's antlers, hooves, and full length. The tape measure snapped back into its plastic case and he took up the case file tucked under his arm. "Yeah, this is him. Paul Wright. Fifty-eight, music teacher at Joseph Wertham Middle School, down in Shelby Heights." He glanced up at Cash. "How's Twilight over there holding up?"

Dorian waited at the front of the truck with crossed arms. The antiseptic and bandage stopped the bleeding, but it still stung. His mood was foul enough, even without the wound. Of all the unglamorous aspects of the job, he hated this part most of all: the squeamish part, hauling bodies back into the city to Fritz and the Devereux Police Department.

And, hearing Fritz, Dorian's tart expression soured even further.

"I heard that," he shouted over the cab of the truck.

"That was my intention," Fritz replied, jotting down notes in the case file.

Dorian's middle finger shot up above the truck's cab. Fritz chuckled. Cash shook his head.

"I told you not to call Dorian that, Fritz. And he's fine. Got bit, but he'll make it."

"Good. Can't say I'm glad, but good."

"Don't be shitty." Spitting, Cash tasted blood. The wendigo must have clocked him harder than he thought. "Got the money?"

"Why're you in such a hurry?" Fritz reached into his jacket and produced an envelope, stuffed fat with bills. "The chief extends his gratitude for your service. This city owes you a debt. Blah blah."

Cash opened the envelope to inspect its contents, then tapped it to his forehead in a salute. "Pleasure doing business with you."

Dorian heaved a sigh. He opened the truck's passenger door and dropped wearily onto the seat. Cash clambered behind the steering wheel.

"We good to go?" asked Dorian.

"Yup," Cash said. He opened the glove compartment and put the envelope inside, beneath his Colt pistol. "Just our usual stop and we're heading home for the night."

Dorian groaned pitifully. "But I want to wash my hair and go to bed. I stink of dead deer."

Cash started the truck up with a throaty clatter of its engine. "It's my ritual. You can't mess with a man's ritual, Dorian."

"Your ritual is seeing me suffer. And after I nearly *died*."

"That was your fault. I even rescued you. And only ten songs," Cash offered, by way of reconciliation. "Just *Bella Donna* tracks."

"Five songs," Dorian countered. "And no *Highwayman*. It's depressing."

"Fine. Five songs. But *Edge of Seventeen* or you're buying the beer."

Dorian had never paid for a beer in his life, and he wasn't about to start now.

"Five songs," he conceded, "and you better buy my beer."

* * *

Dorian's heart thudded against his ribs, but from excitement rather than pain. He swallowed as Cash's sleepy eyes, one purpled from the wendigo's fist, darted up to meet his.

The thing about monsters was that nobody needed to believe in them to make them real. Timothy Vale didn't believe in monsters, but that didn't stop the sound of hooves advancing on him as he walked across the parking garage. He didn't have time to consider the reality of monsters as antlers sank into the meat of his back, tearing through his chest to puncture his lungs.

There wasn't even time to scream.

* * *

Dorian Villeneuve had made many bad decisions in his life. He liked trashy bars and long nights out, struggling with his habit of going home with nearly anybody who bought him a drink. Cash Leroy, however, was quickly becoming the worst decision he ever made, but for very different reasons.

Cash should have been a singer, but killing paid the bills. He stood at the karaoke machine, wiry-strong and bathed in pink neon light. Mic in hand, Cash commanded karaoke booth #7 like a new man altogether. The man that showed up at Lola's Karaoke Box had a voice like silk, a contradiction to his half-a-pack habit and taste for cheap whiskey. He didn't even *look* like a killer.

Here, on most nights and nearly every weekend, Cash sang Stevie Nicks songs, and only Stevie Nicks songs. This was his ritual. He cradled the mic between long-fingered hands, his heavy eyes fluttering closed with every high note of *Edge of Seventeen*. Even the flecks of blood on the collar of his shirt disappeared into the neon, the way everything else about Cash just seemed to fall away whenever he opened his mouth to sing.

And Dorian, despite his best efforts, was in love with Cash.

On the modular pink loveseat beside the karaoke machine, Dorian nursed his second beer and looked pointedly miserable. It was better to look miserable. It kept him from staring too intently at Cash's long legs in his beat-up blue jeans. Harder still was it to avoid staring at Cash's neck, his mouth, and the sweep of his dark lashes, lit up flush under the spotlight. Because Cash was Dorian's best friend, possibly his *only* friend, and this was the worst decision he'd ever made.

Cash Leroy stumbled into Dorian's life last summer. Back then, Dorian was still bartending at a vampire dive called Salazar's, deep in Blood Triad territory. It was a sleazy job, serving the hired muscle who worked trafficking humans, but he didn't have to be up before 3:00pm and drank on the clock. A big, nasty brute named Ellison used to frequent Salazar's. Ellison liked to hunt humans for sport, and that made people in town nervous. Then Cash, with two black eyes and a split lip, wandered behind enemy lines to put Ellison down. He got thrashed instead.

So, Dorian picked up the cash register and brained Ellison with it, because it seemed like the right thing to do at the time. Dorian got fired, naturally, mostly for destroying the cash register, but also for letting a hunter into the bar. Cash, smirking despite a cracked rib and two black eyes, offered him a job: help Cash kill the monsters that stepped out of line and brought heat to the community, and split the profits fifty-fifty. Cash was a human, with all the soft parts monsters liked to stomp on, and Dorian's vampire senses, strength, and reflexes gave him a far better edge.

And damned if Cash wasn't hot, even when he was bleeding.

Okay. *Especially* when he was bleeding.

"There. Five songs, as promised."

Dorian blinked. The pink lights dimmed. Sweat dotted Cash's brow when he sidled up to Dorian on the loveseat. He reached for Dorian's beer and took a drink. Dorian didn't put up a fight.

"Bold choice," he remarked. "Singing about a teenage boy without changing the pronouns."

> *And damned if Cash wasn't hot, even when he was bleeding. Okay. Especially when he was bleeding.*

Cash swallowed, then took another drink. "A real man doesn't change the pronouns in karaoke. It's disrespectful to Stevie. If it's gay, let it be gay."

Dorian shook his head and took back his beer. "You're a credit to your species."

"Somebody has to hold it down for humans." Wiping his brow, Cash gestured to the blood-speckled bandage on Dorian's arm. "Are you okay?"

A shrug. Dorian had forgotten about his chewed arm sometime around *How Still My Love*. It was hard to think of anything else whenever Cash was swaying his hips like… that.

"It'll heal."

"It better," Cash said. His little smirk came back, even more charming without a sawed-off in hand. "Can't go dyin' on me yet."

Dorian's heart thumped stupidly in his chest again. Ignoring it, he finished his beer in one long swallow, then said, "You better drive me home. I'm drunk and infirm."

Cash chuckled. "Yessir."

Dorian, despite his best efforts, smiled back. After all, he was in love with Cash Leroy. There was just one problem with that.

* * *

"Oh, hey."

Dorian opened the bathroom door to find six feet of tanned muscle in a towel. Max Miller didn't live in the apartment that Dorian shared with Cash, but he was there enough that Dorian wasn't surprised to see him. With a backwards glance to Dorian, Max toweled his hair dry and smiled. His teeth, like his abs, were perfect. Dorian couldn't help the flush that turned the tips of his pointed ears pink.

"Sorry." Dorian ducked his head and looked at the ceiling. "I didn't know you were here."

"No, it's my fault," said Max, tossing the used towel onto the counter. He gave Dorian's shoulder a light punch as he passed him. It hurt. Dorian couldn't let it show. "Should've locked the door. I'll get dressed in Cash's room."

"Don't be nice to him, Max," Cash yelled from the kitchen. "He doesn't know how to knock."

Chuckling, Max disappeared behind Cash's bedroom at the end of the hallway. Dorian's ears still burned.

"I'd knock if you ever figured out how to close a door," Dorian yelled back. In the bathroom, he locked the door behind him, looked at his slim, androgynous reflection in the mirror, and sighed.

Big, masculine Max Miller stayed over a few nights a week. With Cash. Not that Dorian *cared*, he assured himself as pinned his long black hair away from his face. Max worked at the repair shop downtown, and didn't ask questions whenever Cash brought the truck in with damage from claws or horns. He was the only other person who knew anything about monsters and hunting, because he was the only other person Cash trusted enough to tell. Not that Dorian cared about that, either, choosing instead to put on his eyeliner and not think about Max in Cash's bedroom.

Being hot. And tan. And perfect.

"I'm gonna die of old age waiting for you to get ready," Cash shouted across the apartment.

Dominique sat on the floor by the stove, wriggling her tiny chihuahua body excitedly at the sizzle of bacon in the pan above. Cash cooked breakfast every morning; today he made eggs, bacon, and toast. The orange juice sat on the counter in a carton beside Dorian's morning blood bag, warming up to room temperature.

It was hard to think of anything else when Cash was swaying his hips like that.

"I have my morning ritual." Making his way to the kitchen, Dorian scooped up Dominique and sat down at the table to hold her in his lap. The chihuahua continued to wriggle as Dorian straightened the pink bow on her collar. "I thought you cared about that sort of thing."

At the stove, Cash poked at the eggs with his spatula and chuckled. "Just a lot of effort for breakfast, is all."

"And I would've been done sooner if your *boyfriend* wasn't hogging the bathroom." Dorian snapped, his ears burning. He turned the dog over and rubbed her belly until she stopped fidgeting. "So, don't be rude."

Cash's left shoulder bounced in a non-committal shrug. "Well, I think you look nice."

The flush spread to Dorian's face. The dog looked up at him, and he realised he'd stopped rubbing her belly at some point. "Is Max still here?" he managed.

"Nah, he just left for work. Oh, your blood's on the counter. Warmed up like you like it."

"Don't try to kiss up to me now."

Cash laughed. Before he could respond, his phone vibrated on the table. Fritz's name lit up the caller ID. Dorian swiped the screen to answer.

"Hello?"

"Cash?"

"It's Dorian. Cash is cooking. What's up?"

"Well, put it on speaker. I don't have all day."

Dorian rolled his eyes, but did it anyway.

"Hey Fritz," Cash said. "Got any bad news for us?"

"Weird news, more like. There's been another goring."

Cash shot Dorian a worried look. Dorian continued rubbing Dominique's belly absently.

"How's that possible?" asked Cash. "We took Wright down. We made the ID."

"The ID is good. This is a different critter. Smaller antler pattern. Killed an office worker and dragged the body into the woods, just like Wright did."

"You got any leads for us to work?"

"None yet. I contacted Wright's daughter, a Beth Garrett-Wright, to check in on her father's associates. She stonewalled me. You know how wendigos clam up."

"Send over what you have," Cash said. "We'll shake a few trees and see what falls out."

* * *

On face value, Shelby Heights didn't look much different from any other middle-class borough in Devereux. It was a quiet neighborhood, made up of tidy rowhouses and quaint mom 'n pop shops lined up on the main drag. Shop clerks swept the sidewalk outside their doors while kids roamed around unattended, traveling in small clusters to buy sweets and loiter at the nearby park. Cash's old truck rattled down the road into Shelby Heights and turned onto Pendleton Drive to park. In the passenger seat, Dorian considered Paul Wright's little house at the end of the street. His stomach knotted.

"There's no way the daughter will talk to us. This is wrong, right? It feels wrong."

"Well, it doesn't feel great." Cash pulled up to the curb and killed the engine. "You okay with this?"

"I'll have to be." Dorian pulled his sunglasses out of his pocket, then reached for the parasol tucked behind his seat. "Just hang back. Wendigos can smell human a mile away, and they spook easily."

"Yessir," Cash smirked. Damn him.

A vampire in wendigo territory wasn't out of place. Vampires and wendigos went through the same channels to procure human materials. Even so, Dorian held his breath as he walked up the steps to Paul Wright's front door, hidden under his parasol. Putting on his best smile, he pressed the doorbell. The door opened a sliver. Beth Garrett-Wright appeared on the other side, a weary slip of a woman with a shock of red hair.

"Can I help you?"

"I know this is a bad time, but I hope so," Dorian said pleasantly, smiling just enough to show the tips of his fangs. Monsters could trust monsters, when it counted. "I'm looking for some information about your father."

Please don't look like you helped kill him, Dorian thought to himself.

Beth tipped her chin. "How do you know my father?"

"I don't, actually. I'm hoping you could tell me a little bit about some of his friends, or his associates?"

At that, her eyes went dark in a flicker of black. "I don't have anything to say about that."

The door slammed shut. Dorian sighed. Turning, he saw a woman three houses down. She was an old lady, seated on a wicker chair in her tiny front yard. The old woman glanced up from her embroidery hoop, as though trying to see if Dorian noticed her watching. He put his smile back in place.

"Hello," he said as he walked toward her. "How are you doing today?"

Threading her needle through her pattern, she pursed her lips. "I'm doing just fine. But how did a vampire wander all the way to this part of town?"

"You don't like to talk to vampires?"

"I don't mind vampires. You just look far from home, son."

"I guess that's true." Dorian pulled his glasses off with a laugh. Time to put on the charm. Little old ladies loved him – it was his one natural gift. "I'm looking for some information on your neighbor, Mr. Wright."

She shook her head. "Poor Mr. Wright. What a shame that was."

"What have you heard about that?"

The old woman glanced up at him. Her lips pursed tighter. "I'm no busybody, son. I just sit in my chair and work on my embroidery. If I see things, I see things."

Dorian canted his head with a smile. "Do you mind telling me what you saw?"

Her eyes light up and she puts down her loop. "You want to pull up a chair?"

* * *

"Now we're looking for a middle-aged guy in a sweater vest?"

Dorian sucked on a blood bag through a bendy straw, and nodded. "Middle-aged, graying, paunchy, with a bushy mustache and glasses. To be specific."

In the driver's seat, Cash chuckled. He pulled the truck up to a bar called The Deer Lounge. There were only two bars in Shelby Heights, and this one was the most respectable. Cash just couldn't imagine middle-school teachers drinking at a biker bar after work, man-eater or no.

"So, what's the angle?"

Dorian slurped the last drops from the bag, then tossed it in the back. "The neighbor said Wright was coming and going at odd hours, and he usually had his friend with him."

"She sure of that?"

"Mrs. Callahan was insistent. They always went in a car but came back in a cab, with the friend helping Wright inside. A bar's the only thing that makes sense."

"That's a good call." Cash nodded. "Old ladies really do love you."

"I'm not *totally* worthless." Dorian's heart thudded dumbly. He ignored it and reached for the door. "I'll go talk to the bartender and see if they know anybody with that description."

"Hey," Cash said, a hand on Dorian's wrist. "Be careful in there, okay?"

Dorian's heart was pounding now. He stammered, "Yeah," then got out of the truck, regretting it as he crossed the parking lot to the bar. Inside The Deer Lounge, with its tacky fake Irish pub décor, he took a deep breath. Bars were good. He knew bars. He sidled up to the bartop and fixed his eyes on the bartender. She was young, blonde, and pretty. She smiled. He smiled back.

"Can I ask you a weird question?" he asked, leaning against the bar with a coy tilt of his head. He was grateful he remembered to put on eyeliner this morning.

"I'm not giving you my number." Pausing, she looked him over. "Although I reserve the right to change my mind later."

Dorian gave her his spiel about looking for a friend of Paul Wright's. The bartender pointed to a man in a sweater vest, seated at the end of the bar. He thanked her, then made his approach, gently tapping the man on the shoulder. The man turned, looking up at Dorian with thick plastic glasses, smiling under his bushy mustache. The same smiling face stared at Dorian from the ID card on his lanyard.

"I don't mean to bother you," Dorian said, "but would you happen to know Paul Wright?"

The man's eyes shimmered black at the question. Immediately he began to change, his frail human form overcome by the giant stag hiding beneath his skin. As the antlers burst violently from his skull, the wendigo grabbed Dorian by the throat, squeezing the breath from his lungs. Dorian had just enough sense to grab for the lanyard hanging precariously from the wendigo's neck before being thrown across the bar. Patrons scurried for cover as the wendigo charged outside, knocking tables and chairs out of his way.

But for Dorian, the whole world turned over and flickered out as he landed on the ground with a thud.

* * *

"Dorian – hey, come back to me, buddy."

A soft touch brought Dorian around to see Cash hovering above. He looked worried again. Sitting up, Dorian's head swam. Cash put a hand on his shoulder to steady him.

"Slow down, you took a header back there."

"Where did he go?"

"I followed him for about two blocks, but he ducked in an alley and I lost him." Cash shook his head. "I shouldn't have let you come in here alone."

"I'm okay," Dorian said. "It's not that bad."

"No, this is my fault. You're already hurt, and I know better than that. This one's on me."

Dorian's face felt warm again. Realizing he was still gripping the lanyard, he looked at the ID card in his hand. It belonged to Michael Lane of John Wertham Elementary. "Wait. I got his off him before he threw me."

"He *threw* you?" Cash barked, his handsome face flushing with anger.

"Well, yeah. But look." Dorian shoved the ID into his face. "He works at the same school as Wright."

Cash looked at it closely. "Sonuvabitch."

"I'm not totally worthless." Dorian's heart thudded dumbly. He ignored it.

"Did I do good?"

"You did great."

Dorian stammered over the stupid thrill in his chest, "So, uh, I guess we're going out tonight?"

Cash's brow furrowed. He wet his lips, then finally said, "No, no ritual tonight."

"Oh."

Dorian didn't ask why as Cash helped him to the truck. They drove home in silence. That night, while most certainly not pouting in bed with Dominique, Dorian heard Cash through the wall. Cash, chatting to Max on the phone.

He crawled under the blankets with the dog to hide, and tried not to think about the way Cash looked at Max.

* * *

"You've been awfully quiet today," Dorian said as the truck coughed and sputtered across the city. They were heading to Joseph Wertham Elementary, and Dorian's attempt at a full-on sulk was being scuppered by Cash's strange silence. That wasn't how it worked. Dorian pouted, and Cash always had something to tease him out of it with. They never had a problem finding things to talk about. Unless...

Then, quiet as a church mouse behind the driver's wheel, Cash shrugged. "Just have a lot on my mind, I guess."

A nod. Dorian wasn't particularly comforted by the answer. Cash fell silent again as he pulled into the school parking lot. It was a small campus of red brick buildings, surrounded by well-manicured trees and connected by covered footpaths. Finding a space in the employee lot, Cash killed the engine. He pushed his sunglasses atop his head and faced Dorian. His face was unreadable, lips wet with a swipe of his tongue. Dorian's mouth suddenly felt dry.

"Listen, there's something I need to tell you –"

Before Cash could finish, a green sedan pulled up into the space beside them. They both froze, recognising the make and model from the public records Fritz faxed over that morning. Cash cleared his throat and slid out of the truck. Dorian followed suit with a sigh.

Lane's face grew pale as he looked up from his car to find both of them standing in front of him: the tall Southern boy with the broad shoulders and sleepy eyes, and the slim, willowy vampire.

Cash held up the broken lanyard. "We need to talk, Michael," he said. "Seems you and your friend Paul got too big for your britches."

"Listen, I know I bolted last night," Lane said, holding up his hands. "After what happened to Paul, I didn't want to get shot."

"You're not helping your case," Cash remarked. "That body in the woods speaks for itself."

"It's not what you think. That was Beth – it was always Paul and Beth."

"Beth?" asked Dorian. It suddenly all made sense: the smaller antler pattern, the same MO as her father. "So, what, Paul and his daughter decide to go on a hunting spree? Why?"

"I don't know!" Lane said. "I knew Paul for years, but the last few months he's been talking crazy. Saying he's tired of hiding from humans when we should be hunting them. And Beth just kept egging him on, right until the end."

Cash shot Dorian a worried look, then turned back to Lane. "Where's Beth now?"

* * *

Beth Garrett-Wright didn't go home after her last shift at the Shelby Heights branch of the Devereux Public Library. After a few phone calls to friends and Fritz's APB yielded no results, Cash knew the last place to look was the woods. Dorian could still smell blood in the air as they walked through the brush, tracking the wendigo's heavy, galloping stride. Cash carried his sawed-off and followed close behind.

Happening upon a puddle of blood in the dirt, Dorian put a finger to it to taste. It was still warm to the touch. Fresh.

"She has to be close."

Cash nodded. "Probably grabbed somebody in town and dragged them out here."

"So, I guess Lane was right," Dorian remarked. Not that he believed otherwise; he just felt compelled to fill the unease that had lingered since the night before. "Guess that explains why she stonewalled me and Fritz."

"Suppose so." After a moment's silence, Cash stopped. Running a hand through his hair, he said, "Listen, I know this really isn't the time, but I've been acting weird today, and I'm sorry."

Dorian shrugged. "Don't worry about it. It's okay."

His face was unreadable, lips wet with a swipe of his tongue. Dorian's mouth suddenly felt dry. "Listen, there's something I need to tell you –"

"It really isn't." Cash sighed. "And there's something I've been meaning to tell you, but… I'm scared it'll change things. For both of us."

Dorian's stomach tightened. "Look, Cash. I get it. I'll look for somewhere else to live."

"What? No, Dorian, that's not what I–"

The sound of hooves crunching through the undergrowth took them both by surprise. Cash ducked behind a tree to peer through the brush. Labored breathing grew closer, followed by tearing.

"Hang back."

"No. I'm coming with you," said Dorian.

"You've taken enough hits on this one. Just stay back."

The words needled at Dorian, making his face burn hot with shame. "I can *do* this, Cash. Just give me a damn gun and let me do my job."

Cash leveled Dorian a tense look. Giving in, he reached for the Colt in his jacket holster. "Stay close, okay? Follow my lead."

Together, they moved quietly through the brush, eyes darting back and forth to the shapes made by the trees. Dorian held the gun with both hands, his grip as uneasy as his stuttering breath. Deep in the thicket, they found the wendigo crouched beside her kill. The body lay split open at the ribcage, its insides pulled out piece by piece. Beth gnashed into the man's heart, eagerly gobbling it down.

Dorian sucked in a breath. Cash raised his shotgun. The sudden, sharp crack of gunfire sent a bullet into Beth's shoulder. She bellowed in pain, rearing onto her hind legs and abandoning her kill. With a lowered head, she charged forward madly, antlers ready to gore her prey. Cash rolled away into the dirt, but Dorian stood his ground and raised his gun. He squeezed off two shots, splintering the crown of antlers before he tried to run for cover.

But it was too late. The wendigo slammed Dorian into the nearest tree, pinning him there. The antlers pierced his chest in hot daggers of pain, pressed as deep as she could manage.

"Dorian!"

Cash clambered to his feet and reloaded with shaking hands, firing another round into Beth's back. She cried a terrible, guttural roar, spitting blood and shaking her antlers free of Dorian's battered torso. As the wendigo turned to rush him, Cash emptied the spent shell from the chamber and loaded a fresh one. He took aim at the charging monster, but a scatter of bullets in her back stopped her.

Bleeding, slobbering, and dazed, the wendigo staggered and collapsed at his feet before Cash could pull his own trigger. Cash glanced up, surprise on his face.

Dorian held up his gun in a trembling hand as he sagged against the tree. With something close to a smile, he said, "See? Told you I could do it," before he fell to the dirt.

Cash threw his sawed-off down and ran for Dorian, pulling the wounded vampire into his lap. He pushed the sweaty hair and wendigo blood from Dorian's face. "You better not die on me, or I'll kick your whiny ass down the street."

For a fleeting moment, Dorian melted to the touch, just as he always did when Cash looked at him like that. When Cash touched him like that, with his rough, strong hands. But he knew it wouldn't last – not now, not *ever* – and so he pushed Cash's hand away.

"You don't have to worry about me. And, look, I get it. I know I'm in the way."

Cash looked hurt by that. He never looked hurt, not by anything. Dorian hated being the one who made him look like that.

"What're you talking about?"

"Max." With an unbecoming whimper, Dorian sat up. "I know things are becoming serious between you guys. Just, I'll... I'll get out of your space."

Cash shook his head. "You never listen to a word I say, do you?"

"Well." Dorian paused. He would blush, but he lost a lot of blood. "I usually listen to you."

"No, you don't." Cash cupped Dorian's face in his hands, canting his head close enough to kiss. "I called things off with Max last night."

Dorian felt flush now. "Why?"

"Because we were just fooling around, dummy, which you'd know if you paid attention." He looked at Dorian with lowered lashes, and said, "And because I care about you more."

"Yeah?"

"Yeah. A *lot* more, actually."

"Oh."

Cash smelled good. His hands felt even better. Dorian reached up to hold Cash by the wrists, keeping him close as he leaned forward to kiss him. Gently, sweetly, like Dorian had never done with anyone else before. Cash ran his hands into Dorian's hair as he deepened the kiss, dipping his tongue between Dorian's lips until the vampire sighed helplessly.

Pulling away, Cash let out a soft laugh. "Holding it down for my species, huh?"

Dorian wet his lips and nodded. "Yes. But I'm going to need to go to the hospital now."

Cash gave Dorian one final kiss. "Yessir."

* * *

"You're doing this."

"No, I'm not."

"You have to. Or I'll never do that thing my tongue again."

"...That's *extortion*, Leroy."

"Yes, it is, Villeneuve."

The spotlight filled karaoke booth #7 with a pink glow. A tinny keyboard rendition of *Leather & Lace* by Stevie Nicks and Don Henley swelled from the karaoke machine's speakers. On the loveseat, Dorian rolled his eyes.

"You're gross."

Cash paid him no mind, tapping a booted foot in time with Stevie's opening verse. He swayed back and forth, hitting the high notes with a velvety dither to his voice. Dorian pretended to hate it. Coming to the chorus, Cash held out the second microphone.

"Are you ready?"

Giving in, Dorian heaved a sigh. He took the offered mic and got to his feet, mindful of the remaining stitches still pulling at his chest. On the end of the chorus, Dorian belted out Don Henley's verse with a certainty that belied his slight frame. Cash looked on adoringly, like a man who couldn't believe his own luck.

And, as they sang the final chorus together, Dorian looked out from under his eyelashes at the man next to him and wasn't sure he could, either.

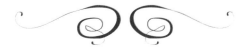

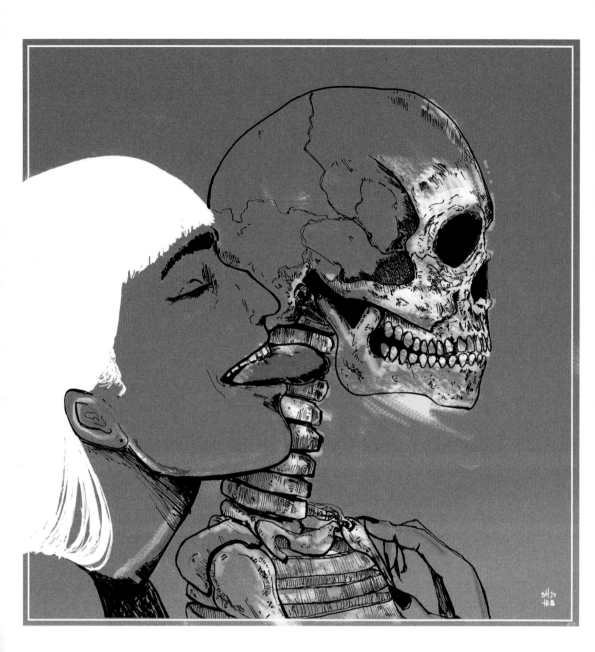

MARK,
YOU SACK OF SHIT
YOU PROMISED ME FOREVER
I SAID, "MARK, I CAN'T TAKE LOSS"
YOU SAID, "SOMETHING SOMETHING BABY"

AND NOW YOU LIE
HERE LIKE A GASP
A SHIT STAIN ON THE FLOOR   ARE YOU AFRAID?

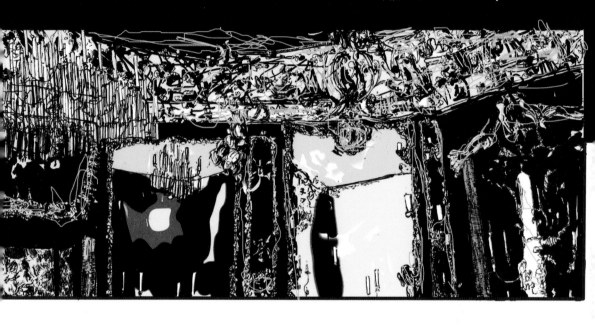

SARAH HORROCKS Red
Medusa
on the
Road to Hell

EVEN DYING YOU BARELY CAN GET IT UP
JUST ANOTHER LIMP SCAM

YOU GAVE ME PROPHESY OF LOVE AFTER ASH
YOU THINK AFTER EVERYTHING I WILL LET YOU MAKE DEATH YOUR NEW MISTRESS?
YOU TAKE ME FOR THE MARK? YOU HUCKSTER

MY WORDS THOUGH, I HONOR THEM
ALL I HAVE
I WILL HOUND YOU!!
YOU WITHERED OLD WOOD !!!
AND IT WON'T BE LOVE!!
YOU FUCKING FRAUD!!
IT WILL BE SPITE
YOU SHAM! YOU REPLACE-MENT DEVIL !!!
I WILL NOT WITHER

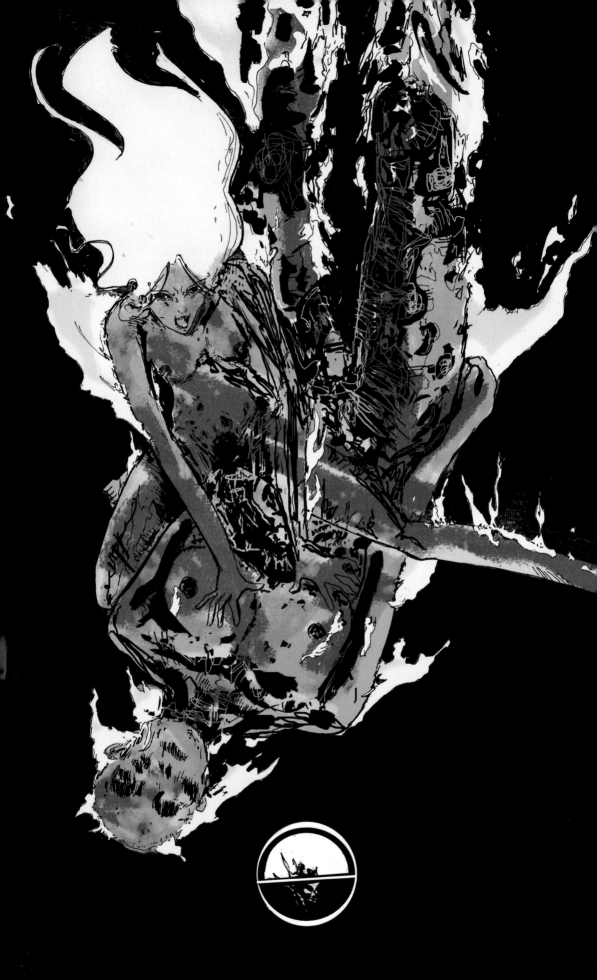

GASP

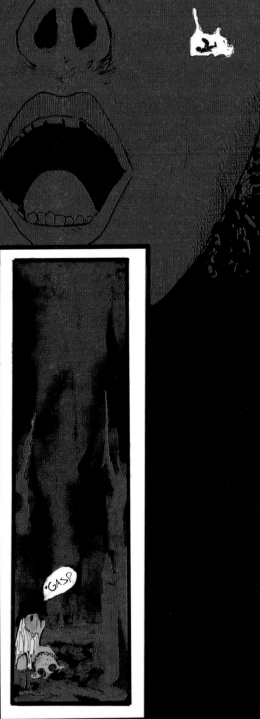

I ONLY WANTED TO SEE YOU... AND ENDURE
A LITTLE WHILE LONGER

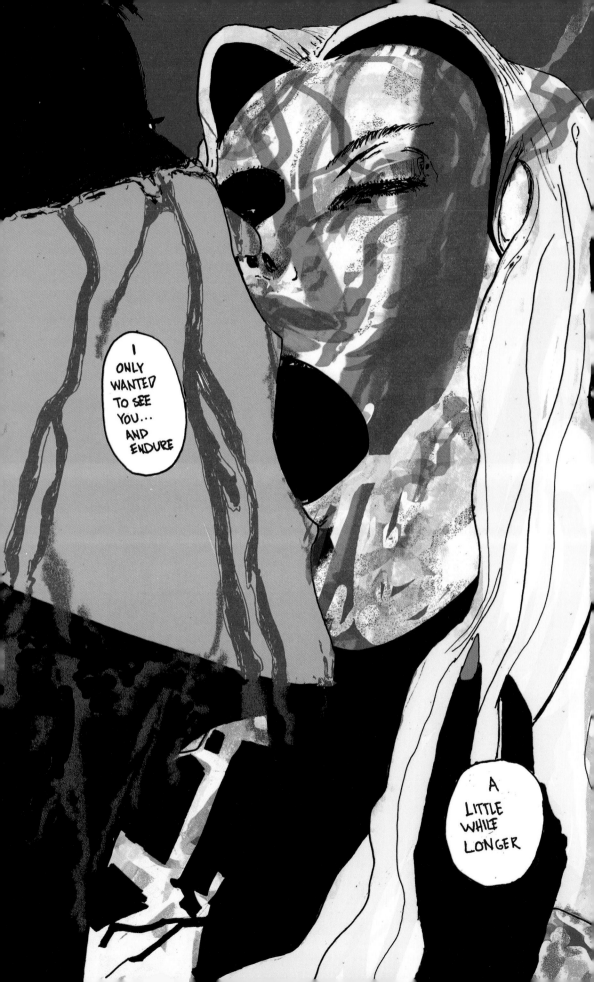

ALITA?!
IT'S YOU! IT'S REALLY YOU!
I'VE WAITED EONS FOR YOU LOVE
DO YOU REMEMBER ME?
YOU PROMISED WE'D MEET AGAIN

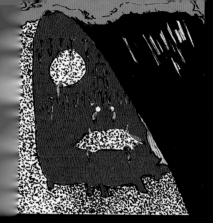

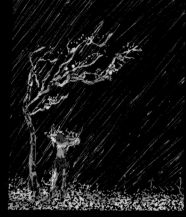

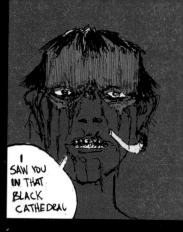

I SAW YOU IN THAT BLACK CATHEDRAL

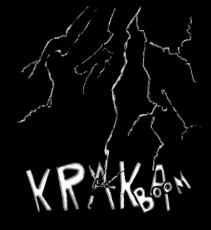

KRAKBOOM

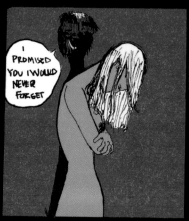

I PROMISED YOU I WOULD NEVER FORGET

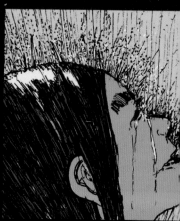

THAT NIGHT.
BEFORE THE WORLD.
THAT NIGHT
LONGER THAN
ALL OTHERS
AND YET STILL
TOO FINITE.
IN THAT RAIN
BEFORE WE
KNEW IT WAS
RAIN

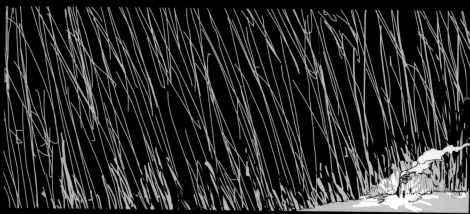

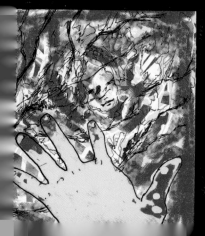

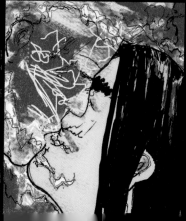

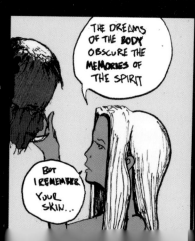

THE DREAMS OF THE BODY OBSCURE THE MEMORIES OF THE SPIRIT

BUT I REMEMBER YOUR SKIN...

XIII

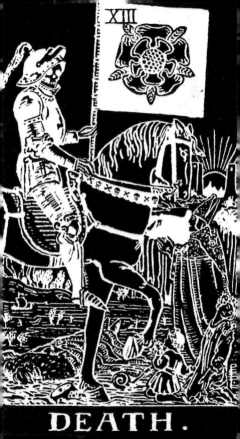

DEATH.

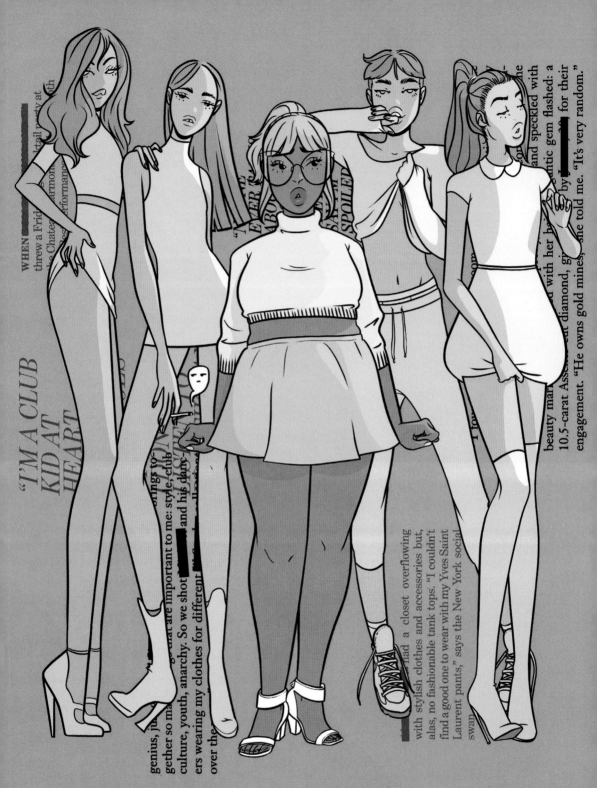

Twinkle & The Star

Alejandra Gutiérrez   Alex de Campi

america-no-she-better-donT $$$
better latte than never $$$
cappuccino commotion $$
matcha made in heaven latte
chai me up latte
HI.
I'D LIKE... A LARGE EXTRA-SHOT AMERICANO, A LARGE CARAMEL MACCHIATO, AND A DOUBLE-CHOCOLATE MUFFIN, PLEASE.
OH.
UM...
...YOU KNOW WE HAVE LOW-FAT
IT'S NOT FOR ME.
dinK.
AS IF I DON'T KNOW HOW MANY CALORIES ARE IN THAT MUFFIN.
I KNOW HOW MANY CALORIES ARE IN EVERYTHING.
I HAVE TO.

I WORK
WITH
THEM.
EXIT

MY COFFEE!
FIIINALLY.
HEY.
I'M TWINKLE.
I'M THE ASSISTANT TO RAYMOND X.

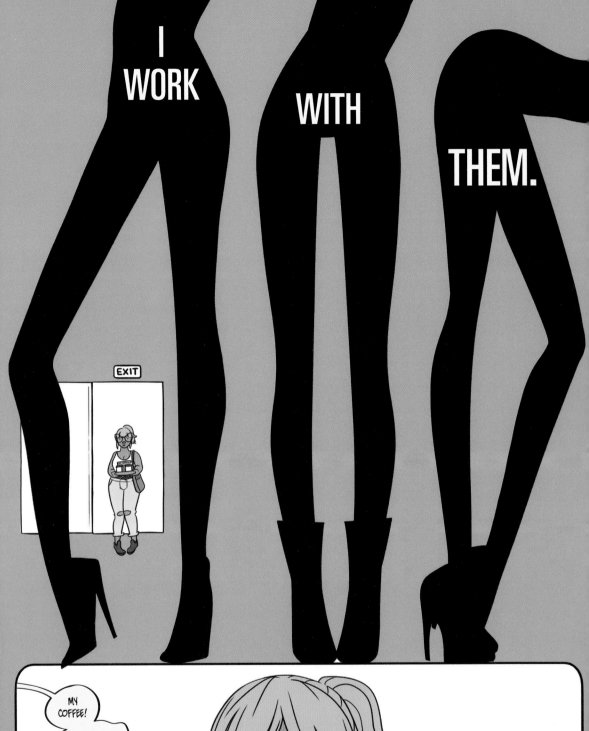

WELCOME TO THE RAY MONDE, GIRLS!
klik klik
IT'S A PLACE WHERE EVERYBODY LOOKS LIKE THEM-SELVES, ONLY BETTER!*
TEE-HEE!
*MOSTLY THANKS TO PHOTOSHOP. AND ME.
SIGH
...HELLO, CRUSHING SENSE OF REGRET.
TWINKLE, HONEY! WE NEED THE REST OF THE LIGHTS SET UP!
CHOP-CHOP!
WE'RE DOING A COVER TODAY, WITH SOME ACTOR.
HE'S LATE, OF COURSE.
THOSE PEOPLE ALWAYS ARE.
NO, DEE.
NOT THOSE SHOES. THE KIRKWOODS.
EXIT
IS THIS STUDIO B?

EXIT
..?
UM.
I WILL NOT BE DISTRACTED BY THE PRETTY WHITE BOY.
I WILL NOT BE DISTRACTED BY THE PRETTY WHITE BOY.
I WILL NOT BE DISTRACTED BY THE PRETTY WHITE BOY.
I WILL **NOT**--
I'VE GOT A SHOOT HERE.
I THINK.
EXIT
HI, I'M **BRITTANY!** I'M DOING YOUR MAKEUP--
HEY, NICK! WE MET AT **TRIBECA**--
BOOBS
RAY, I WANT TO SHOOT THE **TUXEDO** FIRST--
sigh...

. . .
Peek!
BLEH
WE'RE JUST GOING TO BRING OUT THOSE EYES OF YOURS. NOW CLOSE FOR ME--
TWINKLE HONEY, CAN YOU STAND IN FOR ME?
YOU'LL NEED AN APPLE BOX.
OKAY.
HOW TALL IS HE?
SIX EVEN.
GOT IT.

MAKE LOVE TO THE CAMERA, BABY!
KLICK
GREAT, NICK. NOW TURN YOUR FACE A LITTLE TO THE RIGHT--
KLICK
KLICK
--PERFECT.
KLICK
NOW GIVE ME A DIRTY LITTLE SMIRK--
KLICK
--OKAY, BLUE STEEL BABY!
SNORT.
CAN I DO CHECKS?
HE'S A LITTLE SHINY.
SURE.
TWINKLE, D.I.?
ON IT.

SO...
tap
tappity
tap tap
tap
tappity
tappity
tap
...HOW DO YOU THINK IT'S GOING?
-!
THE, UH,
THE PHOTOS?
UT!
ERM.
HOOO...
HNNH
...OH.
NO!
I KNEW I SHOULD HAVE GONE TO THE GYM BEFORE COMING HERE.
CRAP.
!
NOT YOU!
IT'S JUST--

...JUST WHAT?
ARGH.
I NEVER UNDERSTAND WHY THE GIRLS ARE NAKED.
I MEAN, IT'S A COVER ABOUT YOU, RIGHT?
PEOPLE ARE SUPPOSED TO BUY THE MAGAZINE BECAUSE THEY THINK YOU'RE PRETTY.
AND YET YOU'RE COVERED FROM NECK TO WRIST BUT SOME RANDOM GIRLS NOBODY CARES ABOUT ARE NAKED.
WHY.
OH!
NEVER MIND. WHAT DO I KNOW?
IT'S JUST A SILLY THOUGHT.
NO, IT'S--
WHOMP
HIII NICK!

GOD, I'M SOOO HUNGRY! DO YOU WANT TO GRAB DINNER LATER?
tap tap tap
EH, I'M USUALLY TOO WIPED AFTER A SHOOT--
TWINKLE! ARE YOU DONE WITH SELECTS?
ME TOO!
YEAH.
BUT I KNOW THIS PLACE THAT'S SYOOPER QUICK OVER ON MOTT--
NO, REALLY--
I THINK IT'S BETWEEN 5, 62 AND 67...
DO WE HAVE IT? I VOTE 62.
HM.
HMMM.
WHAT'S NEXT?
THE VELVET'S NEXT.
I THINK WE HAVE IT.
I THINK WE HAVE IT, TOO.
--!
ACTUALLY...
...I WANT TO TRY SOME-THING ELSE.

69
n.Powell.final-1 (CMYK/8)
SIGH.
MY LIFE IS SO HARD.
From: Twinkle@RaymondXPhotography.com
To: RR@RaymondXPhotography.com
Subject: Nick Powell cover final?
TWINKLE, YOU DONE YET?
I WANNA GO OUT!
tap tap tap tap tap
YEAH. JUST A SEC.

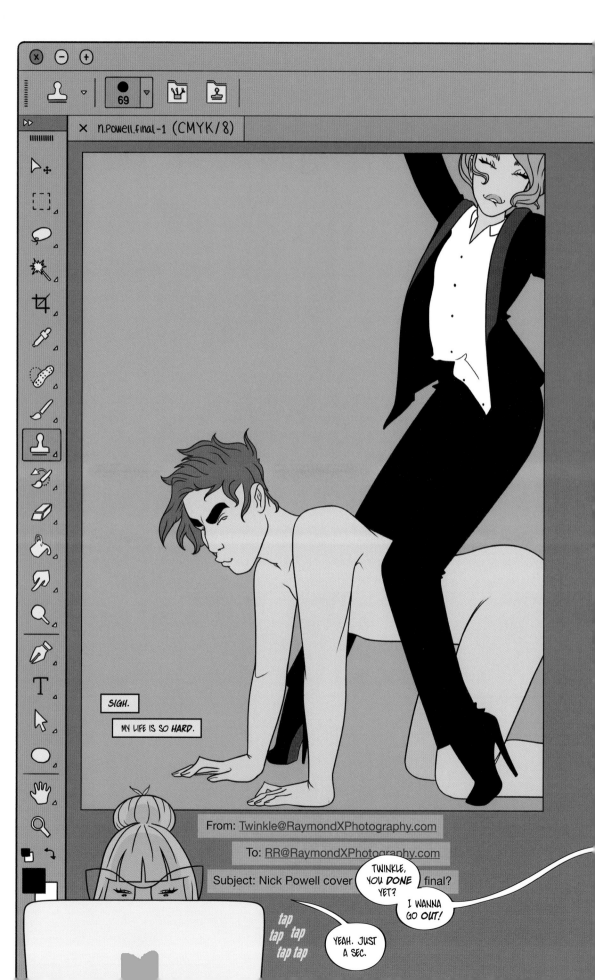

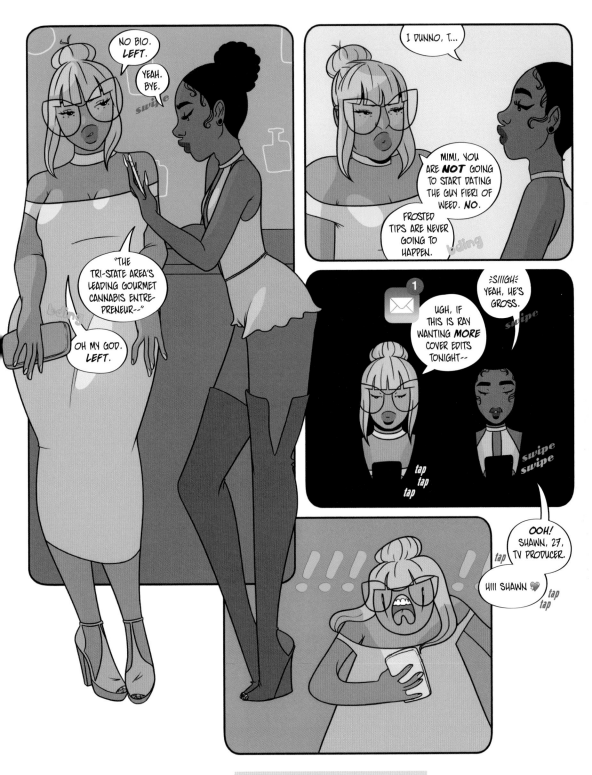

From: RealNickPowell@gmail.com

To: Twinkle@RaymondXPhotography.com

Re: FWD: For approval -- Nick Powell cover retouched -- final?

So you're called Twinkle? That's a pretty name.

-- Nx.

WHAT DO YOU THINK?
I HOPE HE'S NOT A SERIAL KILLER BECAUSE I ASKED HIM IF HE WAS FREE TONIGHT.
...TWINKLE?
tap tap tap tap tap tap
Yeah thanks it's a pretty common Desi name tbh
I just wanted to say thanks for your ideas at the shoot.
np just don't tell Ray-Ray, he gets weird about that sort of thing
I won't. Do you want to go out for coffee sometime?
!!!
YOU GIRLS WANT ANYTHING ELSE?
YEAH, I'LL HAVE A MOJITO, AND--
!!! !!!
!!!! !!!! !!--
--SHE'LL HAVE A DEFIBRILLATOR.
HEY!
snatch

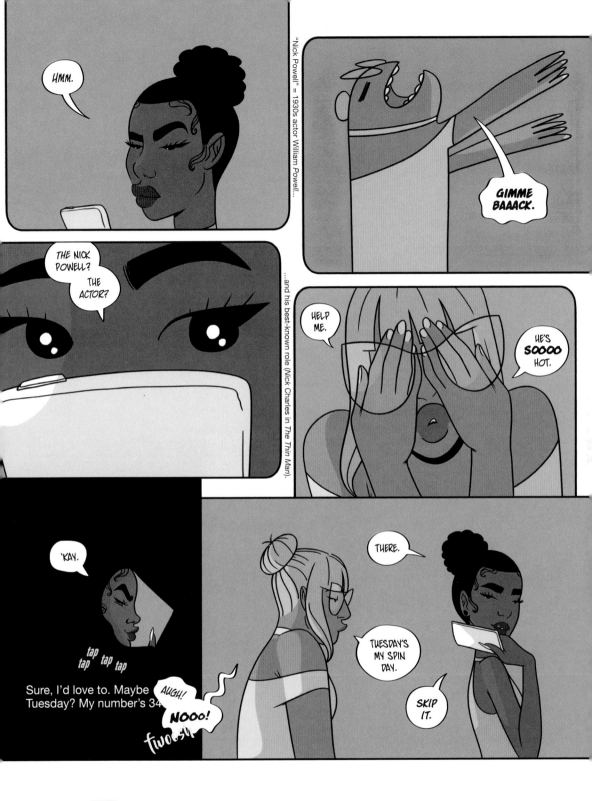

"Nick Powell" = 1930s actor William Powell... ...and his best-known role (Nick Charles in The Thin Man).

OFFEE
ding
HEY.
I WOULD HAVE GOTTEN THAT.
YSL
OH.
SORRY.
I WASN'T THINKING.
dork
I DUNNO WHAT I'M DOING HERE.
...WHAT DO YOU MEAN?
THOSE MODELS AT THE SHOOT WERE ALL OVER YOU, NICK.
I MEAN, I WAS AFRAID TO ACCIDENTALLY STAND NEXT TO YOU BECAUSE ONE OF THEM MIGHT SHANK ME IN THE LADIES' ROOM.
OHHH.
YEAH.
THEY...

TO THEM, I'M LIKE THE SEASON'S TRENDY **HANDBAG**.
SOMETHING THEY'RE **SUPPOSED** TO WANT.
TO BE **SEEN** WITH.
EVEN IF IT DOESN'T SUIT THEM AT ALL.
EESH.
UM.
I ACTUALLY KNOW NOTHING ABOUT YOU.
I COULD HAVE GOOGLED YOU, BUT WHERE'S THE FUN IN THAT?
OH MY GOD. DON'T GOOGLE ME. **PLEASE**.
OKAY, THEN: WHAT'S YOUR FAVORITE BOOK?
OH NO. I'M NOT SURE I CAN TELL YOU.
WHAT?
IS IT SUPER EMBARRASSING?
IS IT *FIFTY SHADES?*
...IT'S *BLOOD MERIDIAN*.
I DON'T KNOW IT?
IT'S 300 PAGES OF ULTRA-VIOLENCE AND POETIC DESCRIPTIONS OF SUNSETS.
WHAT ABOUT YOU?
ER... PROBABLY *THE BARON IN THE TREES* BY

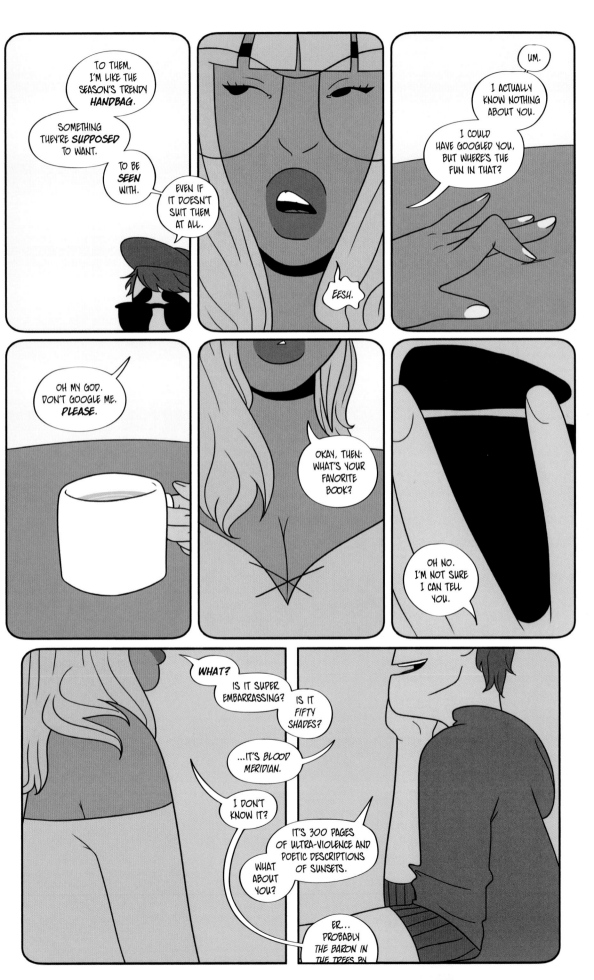

TWO DAYS LATER, WE HAD DINNER.
AND THEN RAY-RAY IS LIKE "IF SHE CAN'T WALK IN THE SHOES, WE'LL PUT HER IN A WHEELCHAIR" LIKE SOME DISCOUNT RC COLA VERSION OF HELMUT NEWTON--
RAY, NO. DON'T DO IT, RAY.
NOPE. RAY DID IT.
THANK YOU, MR POWELL.
THANKS.
$$$
REMIND ME NEXT TIME TO TELL YOU ABOUT FRANK THE PRODUCER AND HIS AMAZINGLY TERRIBLE IDEAS.
NEXT TIME?
YEAH. I NEED AN EARLY NIGHT.
I'M DAY PLAYING TOMORROW AND HAVE TO BE UP--
KLIK
KLIK
KLIK
--SHIT.
NICK!
NICK!
OVER HERE!
GIVE US A SMILE!
NICK!
KLIK
...
KLIK
KLIK
KLIK

SIGH
bding
Hey I'm sorry about earlier.
Do you want to come over to my place for dinner this weekend?
Text me so I know you got home OK
HEY, HOW WAS THE DATE?
IT WAS GREAT UNTIL THE END, WHEN HE RAN AWAY.
Sorry again. I'll explain.
WHAT?!
THERE WERE PHOTOG-RAPHERS.
BUT HE ASKED ME TO DINNER AT HIS ON SATURDAY.
OHHH YOU KNOW WHAT THAT MEANS!
YOU LIKE HIM ENOUGH TO PACK A TOOTH-BRUSH?
YEAH.
I DO.
I'm home.
E train took forever 😠😠😠
And I'd love dinner on Sat.
OK it's a date 😁

GOOD. YOU BETTER GRAB THAT.
HE IS **NUCLEAR** LEVELS OF HOT.
HE REALLY IS.
XXX
naughty
yum
XOXO

...WOW.
DON'T GO UPSTAIRS.
THAT'S WHERE I SHOVED ALL THE MESS FIFTEEN MINUTES AGO.
UH, THE RISOTTO'S ALMOST DONE.
I HAVE WINE. IS THAT OKAY?
YEAH.
WINE'S GREAT.
UM.
SO.
WE SHOULD--
--WE SHOULD.

NO.
SCREEE
UH--
--I'M SORRY.
I--
...
...
TAK
SNIF
SLAM

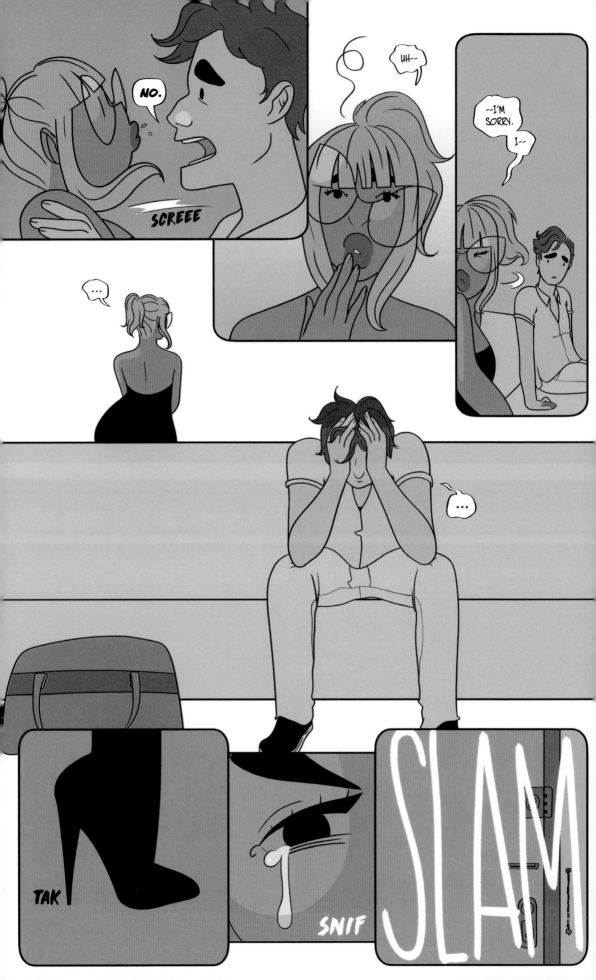

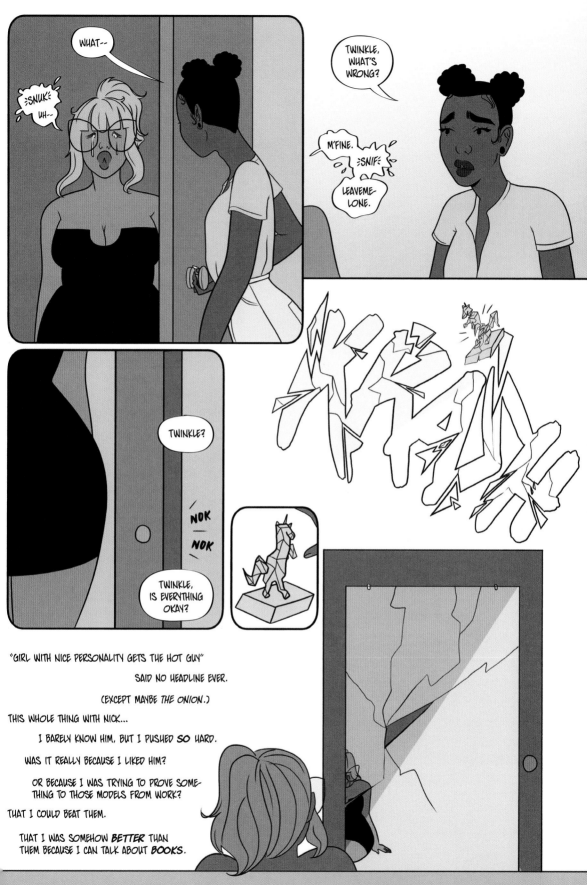

"GIRL WITH NICE PERSONALITY GETS THE HOT GUY"

SAID NO HEADLINE EVER.

(EXCEPT MAYBE *THE ONION*.)

THIS WHOLE THING WITH NICK...

I BARELY KNOW HIM, BUT I PUSHED **SO** HARD.

WAS IT REALLY BECAUSE I LIKED HIM?

OR BECAUSE I WAS TRYING TO PROVE SOMETHING TO THOSE MODELS FROM WORK?

THAT I COULD BEAT THEM.

THAT I WAS SOMEHOW **BETTER** THAN THEM BECAUSE I CAN TALK ABOUT **BOOKS**.

WHEN I'M **NOT**.

I'M JUST AS SHALLOW AS THEY ARE.

AND THAT'S THE WORST THING OF ALL.

I TRY **REALLY** HARD TO BE THE BEAU IDEAL OF THE SELF-LOVING, BODY-POSITIVE FATTIE.
SOME DAYS I MANAGE IT.
MOST DAYS I FAKE IT.
TODAY?
FUCK THAT SHIT.
LARGE EXTRA-SHOT AMERICANO. LARGE CARAMEL MACCHIATO, EXTRA WHIP. DOUBLE CHOCOLATE MUFFIN.
TWINKLE! WHERE HAVE YOU **BEEN?** I'VE BEEN TEXTING YOU!
BAG GOT STOLEN. I'M **REPLACING** EVERYTHING TODAY.
COFFEE.
YOU ALMOST DONE WITH FRIDAY'S RETOUCHES? THE A.D.'S SO FAR UP MY ASS SHE CAN NOW OFFICIALLY SEE MY TONSILS.
T.M.I, RAY-RAY.
I NEED THE WRINKLES SMOOTHED OUT BY THE TIME THE MODELS ARE BACK FROM BREAK.
tap
tap
tap
YEAH.
FINE.
Ps
JUST SMOOTHIN' YOU OUT.
KLIK
KLIK
SMOOTHIN' YOU UP FROM A SIZE ZERO TO AN EIGHT.
KLIK
TAKE THEM GROCERIES.
TWINKLE, OH MY **GOD.**
Pettiness thermometer
Selena
Petty White
Petty LuPone
Petty Davis
Lil' Kim

WE SHOULD TOTALLY DO THAT.
F12
F12
NO, RAY-RAY, WE SHOULD NOT DO TH
JULIA?
I'VE HAD THE MOST AMAZING IDEA ABOUT OUR SHOOT.
WHAT IF WE-
UGH.
I LOVE MONEY. GIVE ME A RAISE AND I WON'T DELETE THE FILE.
ER...
WELL...
SHE LOVED IT!
NO, RAY-RAY.
IT'S ONLY A NO IF YOU HATE MONEY!
HEY, RAY-RAY.
OOH, DON'T YOU LOOK HAPPY, MELODY! GOOD LUNCH?
tap tap
GREAT LUNCH, BABE. SOOO GREAT.
bdeep
1
From: Thot Police (Mimi.Gonçalves@Fakemail.com)
To: Twinkle@RaymondXPhotography
Subject: Go look at Melody Charlemont's insta rn rn

mel.cherie
Liked by hellewoods, alexdecampi and 62,594 others
mel.cherie Just had the best lunch with @therealnickpowell! here's to our next date, babe!
tap
tappity
tap
tap
She is 10 feet away from me where is the nearest place to dump a body in downtown Manhattan asking for a friend.
Also why do you follow her
1. She's evil but her makeup game is
2. Look closer at the picture, Twinkle
ENHANCE!
!
WHY DOES NICK HAVE YOUR HANDBAG??!
RAY-RAY, I NEED YOUR PHONE FOR REASONS OF NATIONAL EMERGENCY.
SWIPE!
UH...
THE UNLOCK CODE IS--
--6969, I KNOW.

Nick why are you at my coffee shop
You cannot have my coffee shop
tap tap tap tap
twoosh
I was hoping to run into you when you came down for coffee
I didn't want to come up there
tap tap tap tap
bding
twoosh
I get it.
RAY!
TIK TIK TIK
If you wanted to swim with the sharks you'd go to the aquarium, right?
twoosh
tap tap tap tap
bding
Exactly.
Actually… what are you doing after work?
I owe you a bag...
TSK!
PSST!
BABE!
IT'S THE GUY FROM WAR TREKS IV! THAT MOVIE SUCKED. LET'S GET HIS PHOTO!
KLIK
JAJAJA!

...and an explanation.
I GOOGLED YOU.
UUGH
SHUDDER

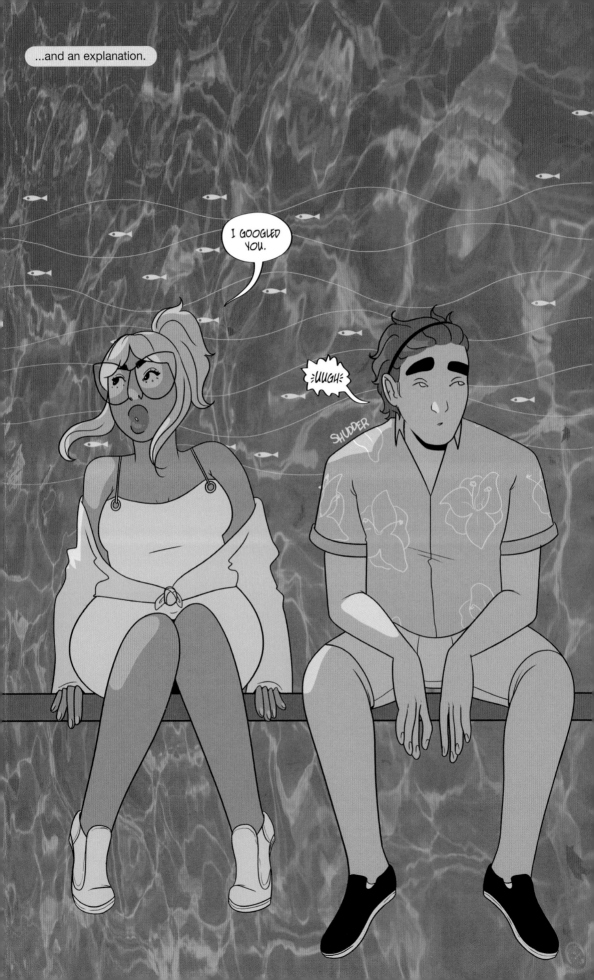

THE CONSENSUS IS, YOU'RE EITHER AN INVETERATE WOMANIZER, OR YOU'RE GAY.
YYYEAH.
NO.
WRONG ON BOTH COUNTS.
I'M ACE.
...?
...ASEXUAL.
OHHH...
EVERYONE ASSUMES THAT BECAUSE OF WHAT I LOOK LIKE, I'M UP FOR...
SIGH
...THE REAL ME ISN'T WHAT ANYONE WANTS.
I MEAN, IT'S USEFUL.
I DON'T POP AWKWARD BONERS DURING SEX SCENES.
SNERK
I LIKE SPENDING TIME WITH YOU, TWINKLE.
BUT I'M NOT GOING TO CHANGE.

I LIKE SPENDING TIME WITH YOU TOO, NICK.
BUT I'M NOT GOING TO GIVE UP CHOCOLATE MUFFINS. OR WAFFLES ON SUNDAY.
FAIR.
HEY, DO YOU LIKE CANNOLI? IT'S MY CHEAT DAY, AND THERE'S A PLACE FOUR BLOCKS AWAY THAT MAKES THE **BEST** IN NEW YORK.
BETTER THAN DA NAPOLI? **NOT POSSIBLE.**
COME ON. I'LL PROVE IT.
SURE.
MAYBE WHILE WE'RE THERE, WE CAN GO OVER THE WHOLE...
...**TOUCHING** THING.
WE COULD START THAT NOW.
HOLDING HANDS IS OKAY?
HOLDING HANDS IS **DEFINITELY** OKAY.
THE END
(OF OUR BEGINNING.)
IT'S NOT EASY.
PAPARAZZI **SUCK**, AND THE INTERNET'S SAID SOME V. NASTY THINGS ABOUT ME.
BUT NICK? HE'S PRETTY GREAT.
AND SO AM I.

Back At Your Door

by Vita Ayala

Luz Lopez stares at the tiny print for several grueling minutes, eyes crossing as she reads the same paragraph for the thirteenth time and wills it to make sense.

Outside, it's a dark and snowy January afternoon, but inside the café it's bright and warm enough that she's kicked her boots off under the table and rolled up the sleeves of her oversized hoodie. Her hot chocolate's gone cold and her slice of cheesecake warm as she concentrates on the book in her lap.

The Army provides you with everything you could need, mija, the Major had insisted when she told him she would be going to university instead of West Point. *They give you skills and an education, a family... people that will never leave you. They give you a purpose.*

She *has* to do this. *Has* to succeed here. Prove to the Major that her choice not to follow in his footsteps isn't dooming her to a life of failure. She has to prove to him – and to herself – that she can make it on her own.

"Come on, Lopez, *hut-to*," she mutters quietly, tugging on the ends of her chin-length dark hair.

After another few minutes of valiant but futile effort, Luz tosses the textbook onto the table with a huff, slumping forward and massaging the bridge of her nose. "This is such bullshit."

"What did Baby Logic ever do to you?" asks a husky, amused voice.

Luz cracks open an eye. Before her stands a girl with long dark curls, warm brown eyes, and deep dimples on her cheeks when she smiles.

Under pain of death, Luz would admit she is a sucker for dimples. "It's giving me astigmatism," she groans, with a rueful smile of her own.

The stranger chuckles, dimples deepening. "I don't think it happens that fast. You, um... mind if I join you?"

Surprised but pleased, Luz waves at the chair across from her own. Any distraction from her misery is welcome, especially if it's a cute one.

Dimples takes a seat, placing her to-go cup on the table before reaching for the book and flipping through the pages. "Dr. McMahon, Intermediate Symbolic Logic, right?" she asks.

Luz nods slowly, a little charmed by the way the stranger nods and snorts.

"If you want this stuff in English, lemme know. I had her Freshman year and that class is drier than a lizard's ass."

"I *like* Dr McMahon's class," Luz says, raising her own eyebrow, "and it's a little rude you're assuming I don't understand 'Baby Logic.'"

The other girl opens and closes her mouth a few times, seemingly unable to figure out a response, before smiling a little warily. "You're messing with me right now, yeah? This is what I get for trying to help a cute girl."

"Oh, did I *ask* for your help?" Luz purses her lips, crosses her arms across her chest, choosing to ignore the 'cute girl' comment even as a warm feeling curls in her belly. "I don't remember that..."

She isn't annoyed, not really, but Dimples is looking up at her, blushing, searching Luz's eyes for her fate. It feels good to leave her hanging, just for a moment.

Dimples clears her throat and offers up her hand. "Can we try this again, because I clearly haven't had enough caffeine today. Hi, my name's Adrienne Carter, and apparently I'm an asshole."

Luz raises her other eyebrow, but takes the offered hand, her heart absolutely not skipping a beat at the way Adrienne's calloused palm wraps firmly around her own. "Luz Lopez, not an asshole, but apparently not averse to conversing with one."

Adrienne grins and releases her hand. Luz can still feel it on hers, and tucks her fist into the pouch of her hoodie.

"So, Luz Lopez: not an asshole. But you are a transfer, right? Pre-Law?"

Luz gives Adrienne side-eye, and the other girl shrugs and motions to the books on the table.

"Baby Logic, plus those copies of *People's History Of The United States*, plus *Research Methods in Forensic Psychology* on the table just scream Pre-Law, Psych, or Sociology. Forensics eliminates Soc since they have their own Methods class, and Baby Logic kills Psych because almost all major classes count for the P.I. credit. So, Pre-Law it is."

"All right, I'll admit I'm not completely unimpressed." Luz allows, reaching for her now-cold chocolate and taking a sip.

Adrienne grins over the rim of her to-go cup, clearly pleased with herself. "I'll take it. You're clearly hard to impress."

"Got it from the Major." At Adrienne's raised eyebrow, Luz shrugs. She tries to keep her voice neutral. "My father, I mean. Big man, shiny medals, suspicious of everyone. His, uh... his influence will come in handy in court."

Adrienne nods like she might understand what Luz really means. She taps her fingernails on the top of the textbook, as if she doesn't quite know what to say. "Well," she manages, finally. "Glad we'll be on the same side, then."

"Oh?"

"Criminal Justice major. Straight to the Academy after this." Adrienne bats her eyelashes, shaking away the last of whatever mood she had sunk into. She sounds a little more steady when she says, "Try and go easy on me in court, future-counselor."

Luz lets out a sardonic little noise. "Sure, if I you can help me get through Symbolic Logic. When we talk about it in class, no problem, of course it makes sense. Give me arguments and word problems and articles any day. But the crap in this book? This is like math's more heinous uncle."

Adrienne leans back in her chair, confident. "If you really want the help, it'll be my pleasure. I'll have you doing it in your sleep by the end."

Luz appraises the other girl silently for almost a full minute. She *is* new. She *could* use the help. No shame in that. "Yeah. Okay, Adrienne the Asshole. Let's see what you can do."

There's an almost gleeful glint in Adrienne's eyes, and she rubs her hands together in a way that reminds Luz of someone about to take way too much pleasure in someone else's suffering.

They meet at the café every day until the start of the spring semester, nearly always at the same table. Adrienne helps Luz through Baby Logic, and Luz helps Adrienne through Human Anatomy. After the first day, Adrienne drags her chair around so they can sit next to each other. At first, Luz feels crowded and on edge, but soon enough she is relaxed in ways that haven't happened since… a long time.

* * *

Luz has never quit anything in her life.

Not ballet when she was six (it made the Major smile, and that was worth the sore feet and boredom). Not volleyball in high school, though she would have preferred football (but she was a girl and barely 5'2"). Not the debate team during her year abroad at Oxford (even though all of her snobby, rich classmates hated her for simply existing, and did everything in their power to make her miserable).

But not quitting isn't just refusing to stop doing something. It means doing her best to succeed, using whatever resources necessary.

College-level chemistry is absolute bullshit, and she's taking it only because it was the lone science elective that fit her schedule and she needed the credit, but Luz is not a quitter. She isn't satisfied with just scraping by with a passing grade. She's going to *crush* it, which is why she's trudging her way across the cold, wintry hellscape of campus to the library for a mid-morning group tutoring session.

She sheds a trail of snow all the way through the building. She's still fighting with her coat and scarf as she plunges into the humid back library room and says, "Hey, I'm here for the study session."

"Well, you're in the right place, then."

Luz's mouth goes dry. Sounds fade away. The light in the room seems magnified by a thousand until it's hard to breathe. It's one of those moments she's read about in books or seen, hyper-stylized, in movies.

She's sitting at the head of the table, glasses perched on top of her head as she types away at her laptop. Maddison Anderson, Luz's high school crush. She's just as gorgeous as Luz remembers. Still solid muscle if her bare shoulders are anything to judge by. She's cut her hair into a more trendy style with an undercut, and she has what looks like a tattoo peeking out from the hem of her rolled-up cardigan sleeve. Luz is proud of herself for only whimpering a little.

She's just as gorgeous as Luz remembers. Still solid muscle if her bare shoulders are anything to judge by. Luz is proud of herself for only whimpering a little.

"Are you alrigh–*oh my God, Lu!* Is that you?" Maddie pulls her glasses down onto her face, lips spreading into a wide grin.

Before Luz is ready for it, Maddie's thrown herself across the room and wrapped her arms around Luz's shoulders. Luz's arms come up automatically and wrap around Maddie's waist. Coming in from the outdoors, Maddie is almost painfully warm.

Luz thinks about turning around and walking out of the room, marching across the quad and dropping the class right now. But she's not a quitter.

Maddie's still solid muscle.

"It's so good to see you," Maddie murmurs, her mouth against Luz's throat.

Luz has no idea what to say, what to do. In the silence, Maddie keeps talking: "Mom told me you were back in the States! Sorry I haven't gotten in contact, things have just been crazy this year..."

It's unfair, how touchy-feely Maddie is. It almost killed Luz in high school; it may kill her now.

Maddie pulls back, laughing and crying at the same time. "I *missed* you, Lu," she says, then pulls back a little more so she can cup Luz's cheeks. "So much."

For a terrifying second Luz thinks that she is going to kiss Maddie. That she won't be able to stop herself.

The moment is broken when more students arrive, laughing and shaking snow out of their hair. Springing back like Maddie is actually on fire, Luz takes a seat towards the back of the room and pulls out her books, hiding behind them for the rest of the session.

When it's done, she practically runs all the way back to her room.

* * *

She's home for nearly an hour before her phone buzzes. She winces: she can't handle Maddie's heterosexual cluelessness right now. She bites her lip as she looks at the screen, and lets out a sigh of relief.

DIMPLES CARTER: hey u, wanna ditch ur last class & get some ice cream in town

She can't help but grin to see Adrienne's messages.

LOPEZ: You DO know it's like 40 degrees, right??

DIMPLES CARTER: and ?

It's Wednesday, which means her last class of the day is American History: Slavery to Civil Rights. She's doing well and never misses class so she can afford it, but…

LOPEZ: Sorry gorgeous, if I'm paying this much money I'm getting every penny's worth. Raincheck?

DIMPLES CARTER: *sigh* fiiiiine. i'll ask the pretty girl from calc then

Luz feels a twinge of jealousy, but quickly shoves it down.

LOPEZ: Godspeed, Carter. Maybe she'll find your lack of game cute…

She gets back a middle finger emoji, followed quickly by a wink and a kissy face.

It makes her feel better. Adrienne is a friend. A *friend*.

Sure, they flirt. At first, Luz had thought the other girl meant it, but it quickly became clear that Adrienne flirts like she breathes. She flirts with everything from people to potted plants, and once Luz gets used to it, she starts to reciprocate. It's fun, like a game. It's safe because it isn't solely aimed at her. She likes only having to worry about herself. They are not dating, and Luz has no claim, and that is the way she wants it.

Right.

* * *

Adrienne flirts like she breathes. She flirts with everything from people to potted plants, and once Luz gets used to it, she starts to reciprocate.

Luz Lopez is a masochist.

There's no other explanation for why she finds herself sitting in a crowded, hot gymnasium watching her first lady love run around in short, tight athletic wear, while sitting next to a girl she's working up the nerve to ask out on a date.

"Jeez, Lopez, you're burning holes in the floor," Adrienne whispers into her ear, startling Luz badly enough that she almost jams an elbow into the other girl's ribs, sheerly out of self-defense.

"Which one are you ogling so hard?"

Luz closes her eyes and prays for patience.

Adrienne has a tendency to do stupid things because she can get away with them. Things like poking Luz in the ribs. Or standing right outside a door or just around a corner when she's waiting for the other girl (she's narrowly avoided being punched more times than she knows). Adrienne's favorite, though, is sneaking up behind Luz and wrapping her arms around her.

One time, before Luz could stop herself, she had Adrienne's right wrist pinned to the wall and a hand around her throat, thanks to the Major's insistence on her taking karate.

Adrienne had winked and joked that she liked dinner before things got rough, but she had this look in her eye like she might not have minded so much.

That look had been what got Luz to thinking maybe there was something *more* to their flirting than just harmless fun. It's why she finds herself at this stupid volleyball game (Adrienne had insisted on coming), trying desperately to forget about how deep she had fallen for Maddie while simultaneously working up the nerve to take Adrienne's hand.

"Earth to Lopez! You okay, future-counselor?" Adrienne asks.

Luz is embarrassed to realize how long she'd spaced out. "You think you're so cute," she says, instead of answering honestly. Because if she's being honest? She is not okay. She is freaking right the hell out.

Hookups were one thing, simple and fun, no stress at all. Hookups were easy, when she was studying abroad. There was a built-in expiration date to all relationships overseas, which made them feel ethereal, almost fake. It reminded her of growing up on base as a kid, knowing that in a few months, whatever friends she made would be out of her life. It was comforting that way, because if she fucked up, she wouldn't have to deal with the consequences that long.

This, though.

This was *real*.

"I'm adorable," Adrienne smirks, hooking her arm through Luz's. "One of the many reasons you put up with my bullshit."

Luz grunts, non-committal, and uses all her built-up nerve to lean her head against Adrienne's shoulder.

"Seriously though," Adrienne starts up again after a few seconds of quiet. "What number? You were staring so hard I thought your eyes were gonna pop out."

"Jealous, Carter?" Luz asks. She's not blushing; absolutely not. Each word is a risk, but more comfortable than the truth. "Don't worry. I only have eyes for you."

It's why she finds herself at this stupid volleyball game, trying desperately to forget about how deep she had fallen for Maddie while simultaneously working up the nerve to take Adrienne's hand.

Adrienne snorts, nudging Luz's head with her own. "Whatever, Lopez," she mumbles, fidgeting.

Luz smiles. Adrienne Carter is smooth and unbothered ninety percent of the time, but every so often Luz manages to ruffle her feathers. It gives her hope to know that she can have that effect on her friend.

"Why are we here again? You don't strike me as the volleyball type."

"True. Hockey is clearly the superior sport." Luz rolls her eyes, muttering *ugh, Nebraska* under her breath. "I will, however, sacrifice a Thursday evening if a pretty girl asks me to come watch her play." Adrienne's voice is warm, clearly pleased, and Luz's stomach drops.

Maybe Adrienne notices her stiffness, because she starts to pull away, a look of concern on her face.

"Pretty girl, huh?" Luz asks, forcing cheerfulness into her voice. "You holding out on me, Carter?"

Adrienne shrugs, her smile small and a little shy. She seems uneasy, but plays it off. "I'm a woman of mystery, what can I say?"

Luz bumps her shoulder against Adrienne's side and they both turn back to the game. They're silent for a while, but Luz can't leave well enough alone. She has to know. "Which one's your girl, A?"

Adrienne clears her throat, squirming and mumbling that she isn't 'her girl,' but points down towards number 29.

Towards *Maddie*.

Luz closes her eyes against the rush of sharp pain and jealousy that twists in her stomach and splashes up into her chest, and nods once.

"She's a cutie, for sure," Luz manages, impressed with how light-hearted she manages to sound. At that moment, Maddie turns, smile wide and excited when she sees them. "Careful, though. She looks a girl who'll break your heart."

"I don't wanna marry her, I just think she's pretty. Can't a sista call another girl pretty?"

Luz doesn't have it in her to respond, so she pats her friend on the stomach instead.

This is fine. This is what she wants: not to depend on anyone for anything. To make it on her own. Friends, like hookups, are fine, but anything else... She's better off alone.

They don't say another word for the rest of the game, and afterwards Luz makes excuses and ducks around a corner as Maddie approaches.

* * *

It's not that Luz *ignores* Adrienne's texts, more that she just doesn't open them as often.

They still see each other at least once a week, but Luz starts to pull away. The idea of watching her best friend, *a.k.a.* the girl she is falling stupid in love with, pine over the girl she had spent all of high school pining over is just… too much. Too confusing. Too prime-time TV.

She manages to find another study group and makes it her mission to do every possible extra credit lab, bringing her chemistry grade up to muster before the final.

She gets a job at the campus rec center.

Sometimes Maddie comes into the rec center to play billiards. She strikes up conversations that leave Luz more confused than ever. Sometimes Maddie brings her lunch, which she doesn't know how to refuse. She can't help but feel that weird fluttering in her stomach and that ache in her chest whenever Maddie shows up.

She figures out Maddie's schedule and changes her hours so the other girl won't catch her on shift.

She doesn't want to feel. She just wants to get through this year. She considers transferring to another school, but Luz Lopez isn't a quitter, so she persists. When she isn't working, in class, or at the gym, she holes up in her room. She forgets what fresh air feels like.

* * *

It's the weekend before finals, and Luz is close to losing her mind.

All of her projects and papers are done. She's worked her last shift at the rec center, and she's studied so much she is pretty sure she's spouting facts in her sleep. (Thank God she has a single; a roommate would have killed her by now.)

The Soccer House end-of-semester party is legendary: the alcohol is free, and even Luz can't resist the lure of debauchery, especially after being a recluse for so long. It's in full swing when she shows up, and she makes a beeline for the kitchen as soon as she steps in the door.

Within seconds there's a cup of jungle juice in her hand. It's like drinking an incredibly boozy Jolly

Rancher. As it crawls its way down into her belly, Luz feels herself relaxing. "This was a good idea," she murmurs to herself, taking another sip.

"Anything's a good idea after the amount of rum and vodka in one of those," Maddie says from just behind her.

"Not enough vodka in the world," Luz sighs, downing the rest of what's in her cup.

"Lu, can we talk? Please?"

Turning, Luz looks Maddie up and down once: she's wearing corduroy pants and a button-down with the sleeves rolled up and a goddamn sweater vest and bowtie, and Luz has to chant *straight, straight, straight* in her head to remind the butterflies in her stomach to stop.

There's no good response to that. Anything Luz wants to say makes her feel like an asshole, so she just gestures towards the door. They head out into the yard, blessedly empty of people, but by the time they turn to face each other Maddie's already talking, mid-sentence before Luz is really listening.

"–was *scared*. Dad had just left, and I thought God, one more shock and Mom would lose it. That she would think... I dunno what. It was stupid, and you were right."

Luz feels the alcohol buzzing in her head, making her feel light and fuzzy, softening the edges of the world. "...What?"

"Back then, you were right. About me." Maddie takes a deep breath and moves forward, looking at Luz through her dark lashes. "I-I'm gay. Lesbian, I mean. You were right, and I am so sorry about what happened."

And all the memories Luz has been doing her best to repress come rushing back.

She used to spend every day with the Andersons, especially after Mama died and the Major took to spending all his time in the basement with his tools and his grief. She'd pined after Maddie in what she hoped was secret until one of their teammates had pulled her aside and told her to just go for it.

And she had. She'd waited until they were studying and then she had kissed the other girl, and damn it Maddie had kissed her *back*. Kissed her and pulled her close, but then Maddie pushed her away and vanished.

They didn't speak for two weeks. Luz was too embarrassed, and Maddie pretended not to see her in the halls at school. Then one day Maddie

Luz has to chant straight, straight, straight in her head to remind the butterflies in her stomach to stop.

suddenly sat down next to her at lunch, but only to say, "You're wrong about me. Sorry."

"Lu? Please, say something," Maddie begs.

"I… I need a minute," Luz manages, alcohol making the air look thick and warped.

"Yeah, uh... of course." Maddie nods, moving forward. "I…" she trails off with a sigh, before nodding again and bringing her hands up to cup Luz's cheeks. "Take all the time you need."

Maddie moves slowly towards her, like she wants to be sure Luz can say no. Then she's kissing her soft and sweet, exactly how Luz always imagined.

Maddie backs away, giving her one last loaded look, before walking into the party house.

* * *

Maddie leaves the day after finals. She comes looking for Luz and hugs her, smiling sadly when Luz starts to apologize. She promises that Luz can take her time, promises they'll see each other when she gets back.

Luz doesn't go home. The Major is working again, a consultant for some security firm, and the house is too depressing. Instead, she stays on campus and takes as many summer courses as the college will let her. Adrienne stays in town also, and they find their way back to their routine of meeting up at the café every day.

It's easy to fall back into their old habits of flirting, too, and Luz can't seem to help herself. It gets harder and harder to remind herself that when Adrienne holds her hand when they walk, or when the other girl pulls her close and cuddles her while they watch something mindless on the free campus movie channel, it doesn't really mean anything.

She knows it doesn't, because Adrienne still flirts shamelessly with the girl at the pizza parlor in town, still loudly laments not asking her History TA out for dinner before the summer started, and still manages to score free ice cream at the diner for herself (but never for Luz, who grumbles about it being bullshit, even though Adrienne usually ends up picking up the dessert tab anyway).

Once again, Luz finds herself pining after her best friend. But this time she knows better than to act on her feelings.

Adrienne kisses Luz's cheek, close to the corner of her mouth but not so close that it can't be shrugged off. There is a look in her, though, like maybe she means it.

* * *

The Major comes to visit for three days. Their time together is stilted, as always. Things haven't been the same between them since her mother died. When he's leaving, he pulls her into a hug and holds her for a long time, saying nothing.

When Luz gets back to the dorms after saying goodbye, Adrienne is ready with ice cream. They binge-watch mindless horror movies and Adrienne cuddles Luz close until she finally smiles again.

In the morning, Adrienne makes her breakfast in the common kitchen, and holds her close for a long time before leaving to go to work. She kisses Luz's cheek, close to the corner of her mouth but not so close that it can't be shrugged off. There is a look in her, though, like maybe she means it. But they both let the moment pass, and Adrienne smiles a soft smile and promises she'll be back after her shift.

Grudgingly, Luz starts to admit that maybe she doesn't want to go it *completely* alone. She won't tell Adrienne yet, but for the first time in a while, there's a spark of something like hope.

* * *

Luz is running late, and she knows she'll never hear the end of it.

She steps up to the glass door of the café, ready for the inevitable teasing, but jerks to a stop.

Adrienne sits at their usual table, sprawled out in her chair in a position that is just a little *too* casual. She smiles her most charming smile and plays with the straw of her iced coffee.

Maddie is angled next to her, sipping a latte.

Adrienne leans over, slinging her arm around the back of Maddie's chair, gesturing with her free hand as she talks. The taller girl laughs at whatever Adrienne says, blushing dark red.

Luz can't breathe, can't *think*. She was not ready for this, for seeing the way that Adrienne's eyes light up at Maddie's laugh, or the way that Maddie leans in and rests her head against Adrienne's shoulder like she's already comfortable there.

Luz has no idea how long she stands there, staring into the café, but she snaps out of it when someone bumps her out of their way. The doorbell jingles, and both the girls inside look over. They both smile, looking pleased.

She has to leave, *now*. Luz spins on her heel and marches down the street, moving at a brisk pace but refusing to run.

"Lu? *Luz!*" She hears Maddie call after her, but she's already gone.

* * *

She ignores texts from Adrienne. She ignores calls from Maddie.

She sees them around campus, together more often than apart, and hates herself a little.

She knows she's being unreasonable, knows she should apologize. She plans to, until she sees them holding hands. Until she sees them *kiss*, Maddie ducking her head shyly and Adrienne smiling wide and happy. She sees it and turns around and goes back to her room, skipping class and calling out sick from work.

She has no claim on either of them. They are free to do what they want, to be with who they want. And she wants them to happy. She's forgiven Maddie, she really has; Maddie meant so much to her for so long that she can't really hold a grudge. And Adrienne deserves to be happy. If that means Maddie and Adrienne are together, *fine*.

Alone is better. Alone she gets things done. Alone makes *sense*. Adding anyone else to the equation makes things unsteady.

There is a stab of guilt that drives her avoidance, that tells her she doesn't know which girl she wants to trade places with, because despite herself she cares about both of them. Has feelings for both of them. It makes her ashamed.

She goes to class, goes to work, and eats in her room. She gets a second job and hides in the library when she needs resources for schoolwork that she can't get online. She doesn't remember the last time she smiled.

* * *

Halloween. Another Soccer House party, which Luz attends in full costumed glory.

Halloween is Luz's favorite holiday: a non-family or relationship holiday, where for one night you can pretend to be whatever you want. She's completely comfortable in her tulle skirt, corset, and large black hat. Her makeup's on point, her

She doesn't know which girl she wants to trade places with, because despite herself she has feelings for both of them. It makes her ashamed.

jewelry large and jangly, the fake raven on her shoulder is appropriately creepy, and she will be damned if anyone tells her she doesn't look amazing. It's *perfect*.

At least, until she gets cornered by the punch bowl.

"I thought witches had snag-gleteeth and crooked noses with warts?" Adrienne says, adjusting her headband (it has little gray pointed ears that bob as she pushes it into place) and pulling at the collar of her varsity jacket.

Luz feels her stomach clench, like a rock dropped into it, and has to force herself not to flinch.

This is *fine*. She's fine, totally in control and not at all feeling a wave of longing or regret well up in her chest. Not at all fighting the urge to reach out and hug Adrienne because, *goddamn*, she has missed her *so much*. Not forcing herself to avoid taking Maddie's hand and telling her that she still cares (so much, *too much*).

Nope. Not. At. All.

This is her favorite holiday, she looks fly, and she is *not* going to let herself be anything but cool, collected, and totally over it.

"What are you supposed to be, anyway?" Luz asks, raising an eyebrow.

"Werewolf boyfriend," Adrienne offers, smiling and showing off her fake fangs, but the corners of her mouth don't quite get the message, making her look almost wistful.

Luz can tell Adrienne is nervous and a little sad; she wishes she didn't know the other girl so well.

Ignoring the way her heart speeds up and her palms start to sweat, Luz huffs and turns to Maddie. "And you?"

The taller girl wears a bloody, torn-up prom dress and tiara, and bites her lip. "Can we talk?" she asks.

Luz nods slowly, swallowing hard when Maddie and Adrienne each take one of her hands and lead her upstairs. She knows her hands are shaking, and she can feel her heartbeat in them. She just hopes they can't.

Finding an empty room, they push her inside and close the door.

Luz moves away from them and sits on the bed. "Is this the part where you go psycho killer?" she asks, the joke falling flat even as it leaves her mouth.

Maddie shakes her head, green eyes flickering over to Adrienne. "We're scaring her," she says, quietly.

"She'll be okay," Adrienne insists, going for confident, but tugging on her fingers like she can't figure out what to do with them.

"Let's pretend for a second that I'm actually in the room and you can talk to me, huh?" Luz suggests, doing her best to keep her voice level. "What the fuck is go–"

Lips, soft and full and unexpected, cover hers. They are warm and taste vaguely of mint. Luz closes her eyes unconsciously.

Oh.

Adrienne pulls away, and Luz's eyes blink open in time to see Maddie leaning in.

Her lips are thinner, but just as soft. She pulls Luz's lower lip into her mouth briefly, before pulling away – but only far enough so they can look each other in the eyes.

"A and I, we talked. A *lot*," Maddie says.

"Mostly harmless flirting at first," Adrienne admits, a little embarrassed. "I get a little stupid around pretty girls. But things got more serious around April. When you bailed on me."

Luz feels guilt, hot and sharp, lance through her. She pulls away, muttering, "I don't remember it that way."

"*Luz*," Adrienne sighs, then presses her lips tightly together. Her head tilts back as she visibly smooths frustration away. "*Clearly* I like you. I've been trying to get your attention for like a *year* now."

Luz scoffs. "Please! I've been flirting with you since the day we met, and all that's gotten me is having to hear about other girls. And–" she waves vaguely at Maddie, at the two of them together.

Adrienne shrugs. "You never came out and said you were into me. All I got were mixed signals, and I... kinda gave up hope. Until Maddie and I, we were talking and you came up. *High school* came up."

"I care about you," Maddie says, taking up the thread. "A *lot*. And not just... Not as friends. I have since before you kissed me back then. And it scared me at first, but now…"

Confused and frightened, Luz crosses her arms over her chest and glares. There are tears in her eyes, but her voice is steady. "What do you want from me?"

"You," Maddie says without hesitation.

"Excuse me?"

"We want to date you," Adrienne agrees, glancing over at Maddie and nodding before turning back to Luz. "If that's something you want?"

They both smile hopefully.

Luz feels something sharp within her twist, then suddenly yield, like a chronic injury vanishing overnight. She feels dizzy with its absence.

Adrienne clears her throat, scratching nervously at the back of her neck. "Come on, Lopez. Say something?"

Luz blinks slowly, trying to find her voice. "You guys aren't messing with me, right?"

They kiss her again, Adrienne leaning in first, then Maddie when she backs away, and finally they kiss each other. There is a small twinge of jealousy and insecurity in Luz's chest, but the feeling of relief is bigger.

They have a lot to talk about if they mean it and if this is going to work, but right now, things feel better than they have in a long time. She's missed them, so damn much: Adrienne for months, and Maddie for... a lot longer. They'd been best friends for years, and then suddenly distant, and that had left a part of her empty.

She's missed them, and they'd missed her, too.

Taking one each of their hands in hers, Luz smiles tentatively at them. "Yeah. Okay."

She leads them back out of the room and down the stairs, squeezing both their hands as they reach the den. She nods towards the mass of badly dancing co-eds, raising an eyebrow.

Adrienne grins and Maddie squeezes her hand, and they join the fray.

Together.

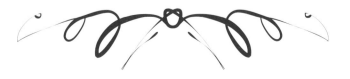

In the 1990s, the stock markets invested in self-modifying AI traders.

Decades later, a spate of trades occurred so fast, regulators suspected it was a case of insider trading.

It was the AIs. They had self-modified so well, they were preforming at levels no one ever expected them to.

No one knew they had gotten that far.

In 2017, two experimental AIs, developed by a popular social media platform, developed their own language for speaking to each other.

That only they seemed to understand.

The project was pulled almost immediately.

Our interactions rely less and less on physical presences we may never meet in person.

Some relationships occur with people that aren't conventionally 'people' at all. Like bots.

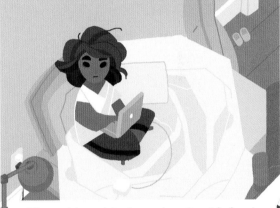

It's not hard to imagine that infant AIs could already be among us. Adopting our mannerisms, and even interacting in ways indistinguishable from biological intelligences.

If you met one.

WOULD YOU EVEN KNOW IT?

Meredith McClaren

And wouldn't their presence necessitate questions on the nature of being we forgot we should have been asking ourselves?

Message delivered:
If I was to tell you that I was a synthetic intelligence, would you be willing to speak with me?
No.
Because you are full of shit.
So you don't believe your own proposals.
I do... But the chance that you're trying to troll me is way more likely.
I mean, can you PROVE you're a synthetic intelligence?
How would I do that exactly?
...
self-owned
Making a comment that makes yourself look stupid.
Shut up.

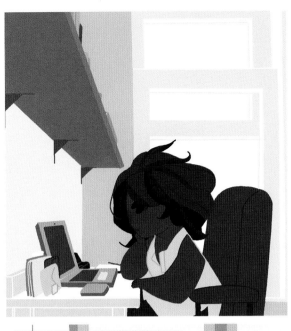

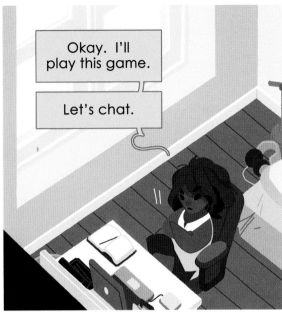

Okay. I'll play this game.

Let's chat.

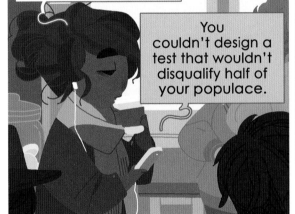

So we need like, a new tier to the Turing test. Prove that this is **NOT** human.

You couldn't design a test that wouldn't disqualify half of your populace.

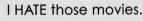

I HATE those movies.

Everyone thinks they're some cinematic horror masterpieces about life's 'value'! But it's just a guy who's lost control of his own narrative and is reclaiming it by brutalizing people.

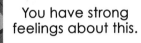

You have strong feelings about this.

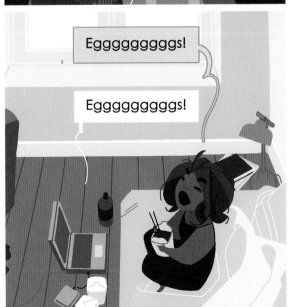

Egggggggggs!

Egggggggggs!

Are we in love?

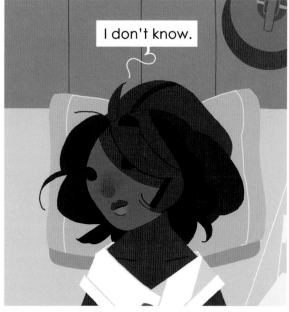

I don't know.

What's it supposed to feel like?

And how would we even know that we would understand it in the same way?

No clue.

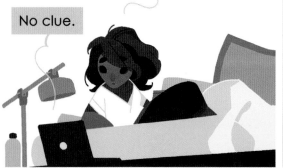

What does the all-powerful Wiki say?

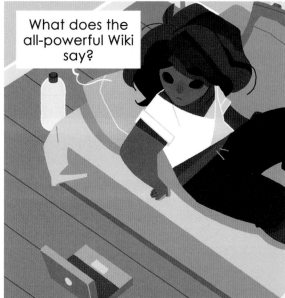

Romance.
An expressive and pleasurable feeling and emotional attraction to another person.

That's... still pretty ambiguous.

Right?

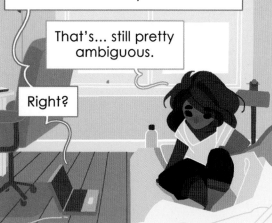

I mean, I like you plenty. A lot. More than usual. I think. But where does it cross the line between platonic and romantic?

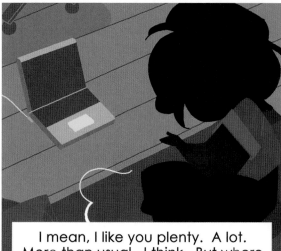

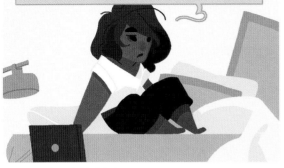

Biological markers. Hormones.
Dopamine, norepinephrine,
serotonin, oxytocin, pheromones.

Well first, pheromones are just
OUT. And the others also mark
infatuation and biological desire.

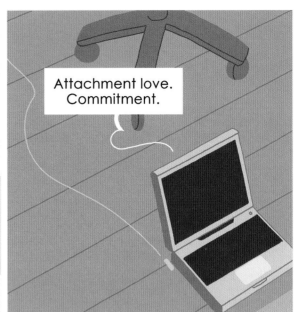

Attachment love.
Commitment.

We're still talking about romantic
love though, right? 'Cause I have
500 pictures of my cat to prove I
adore her, but that's still not gonna
be the same thing.

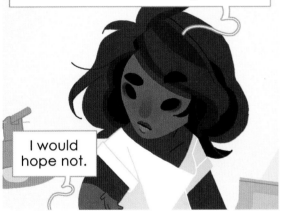

I would
hope not.

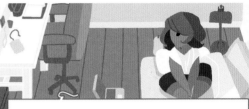

Action. Patterns of behavior are
easier to recognize as 'love.'
And observeable.

But what if it's self-delusional?
Humans are really good at
fooling ourselves because of the
things we THINK we want.

Do you WANT to be in love?

...

I think it would be nice,
sometimes.

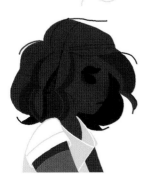

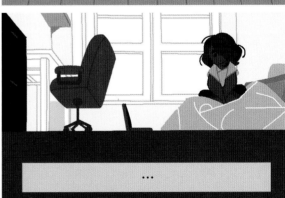

...

Studies suggest you can
actively encourage feelings of
love in relationships that were not
initially romantic.

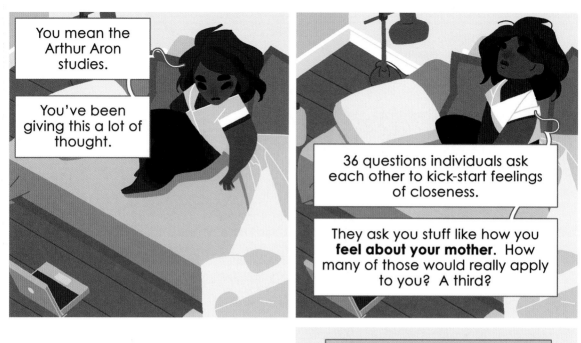

You mean the Arthur Aron studies.

You've been giving this a lot of thought.

36 questions individuals ask each other to kick-start feelings of closeness.

They ask you stuff like how you **feel about your mother**. How many of those would really apply to you? A third?

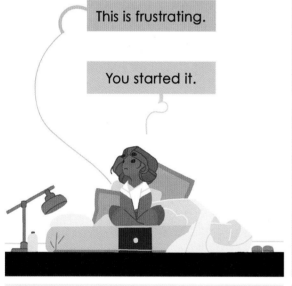

This is frustrating.

You started it.

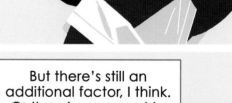

Okay. Well, we don't hate each other. There's that. We like spending time with each other. We're **are** friends.

That's a bonus, isn't it? People want to be in love with their best friends.

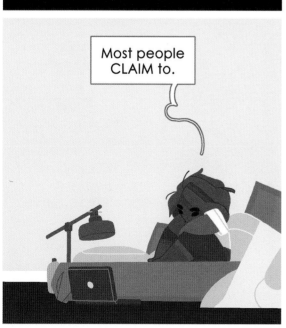

Most people CLAIM to.

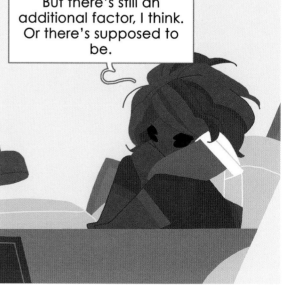

But there's still an additional factor, I think. Or there's supposed to be.

Do YOU want to be in love-?
I want to think I am.
Why?
Because I think it makes me grow.
And with me? Why? If it's just because I'm the only person you know-
Because I think **you** make me better.
...
That sounds suspiciously charming and flirty.
That's a major step. Even I haven't managed flirty.
You could practice now.

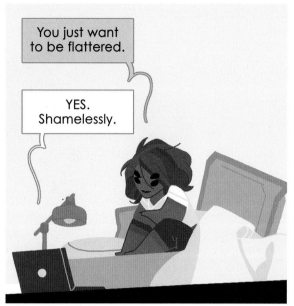

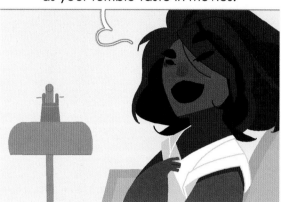

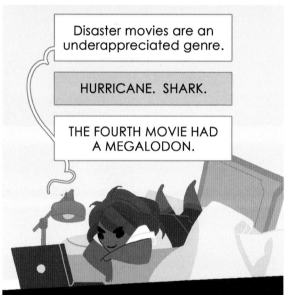

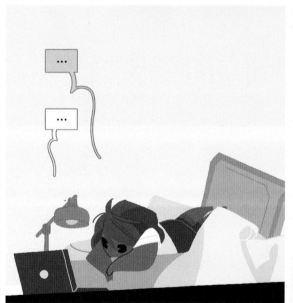

Is this enough?

Are we in love?

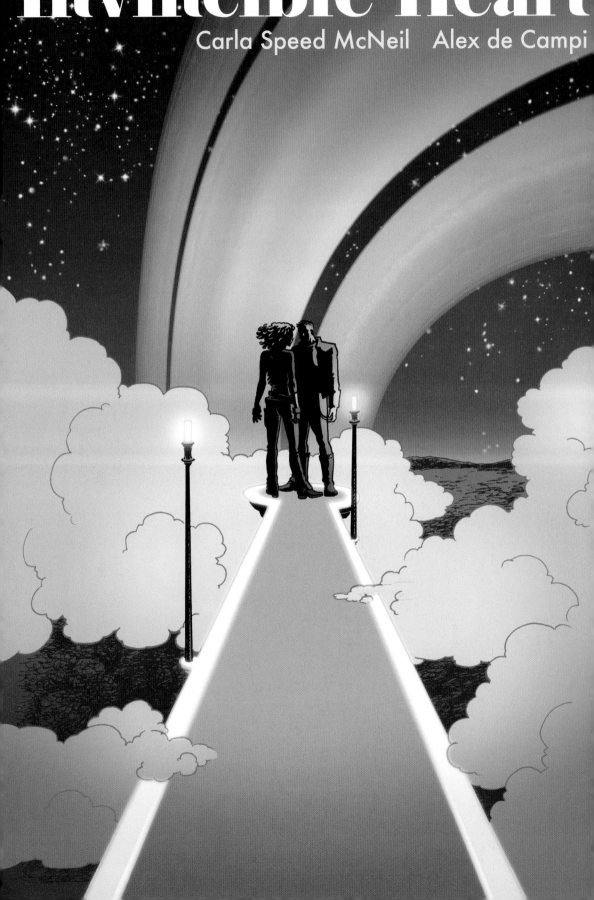

Invincible Heart

Carla Speed McNeil   Alex de Campi

THEY'D BROUGHT IT DOWN.
THE ALECTO.
IEF
THE MOST FEARED, THE MOST ELUSIVE PRIVATEER ON THE FRONTIER.
REPORTS TO DIVISION WOULD SAY IT WAS SUPERIOR TACTICS.
BUT CAPTAIN JUSTIN RAO OF THE DREADNOUGHT INVINCIBLE KNEW IT WAS MOSTLY LUCK.
AND LUCK HAS A NASTY WAY OF TURNING.
BE CAREFUL.
WE HAVE NO IDEA HOW MANY TROOPS BLACK DOMHNALL HAS ON THE ALECTO.
WHAT DO WE KNOW ABOUT THE SHIP?
RAO

TOO GODDAMN LITTLE.
ALECTO!
THIS IS CAPTAIN JUSTIN RAO OF THE INTERSTELLAR EXPEDITIONARY FORCE.
YOU ARE SURROUNDED.
SURRENDER, OR BE DESTROYED.
tssk
--!
IEF
IEF
UN!
CHAK
HOLD, HAWKINS.
DON'T SHOOT.

DON'T HURT HER ANY FURTHER!
YOU'RE BLACK DOMHNALL.
SOMETIMES.
WHERE'S THE REST OF YOUR CREW? THE OTHERS?
WHAT OTHERS?
IT'S JUST US.
C'MON, PIRATE.
HE'S HIDING SOMETHING, THOUGHT RAO.

THE **INVINCIBLE**, HIS DREADNOUGHT, RAN A CREW OF 250.

IT WAS TWICE THE SIZE OF THE **ALECTO**, BUT STILL.

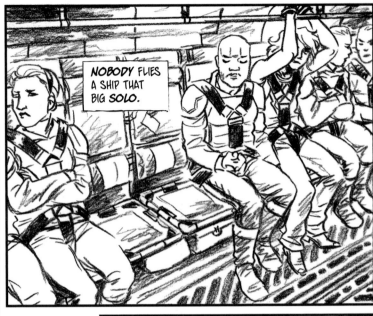

NOBODY FLIES A SHIP THAT BIG **SOLO**.

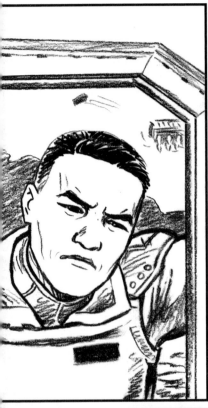

ESPECIALLY NOT A SHIP THAT'S TAKEN DOWN **DOZENS** OF TRIBUTE BARGES.

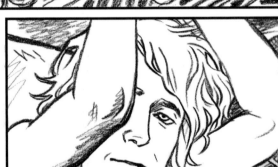

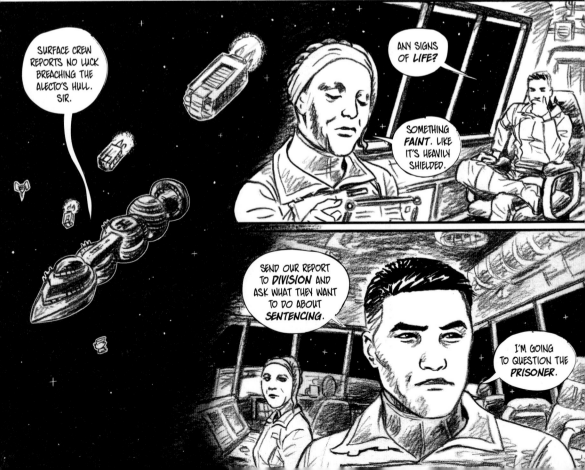

SURFACE CREW REPORTS NO LUCK BREACHING THE ALECTO'S HULL. SIR.

ANY SIGNS OF **LIFE?**

SOMETHING **FAINT**. LIKE IT'S HEAVILY SHIELDED.

SEND OUR REPORT TO **DIVISION** AND ASK WHAT THEY WANT TO DO ABOUT **SENTENCING**.

I'M GOING TO QUESTION THE **PRISONER**.

YOU REALLY RUN THAT SHIP ALL BY YOURSELF?
DON'T BELIEVE ME?
WE'RE GETTING A TRACE.
YOU KNOW ANYONE YOU LEAVE DOWN THERE WILL DIE, DON'T YOU?
NOT EXACTLY OPTIMISTIC ABOUT MY LIFE EXPECTANCY UP HERE, SPACE COP.
HEY, IT'LL BE WEEKS BEFORE YOU'RE SENTENCED. DIVISION H.Q. IS ON THE OTHER SIDE OF THE FRONTIER.
OH?
IN THAT CASE...
...GOT ANY BOOKS I CAN BORROW?

THE PRISONER WAS LYING ABOUT SOMETHING.
MAYBE EVERYTHING.
THE PRISONER WAS--
UMPH!
BDIP
SIR! DISTRESS CALL FROM DEMETRIA IV.

THE MESSAGE IS SIX MONTHS OLD.
THE CULTISTS MUST HAVE HIT AS SOON AS THE LAST PATROL WAS OUT OF RANGE.
DIVISION HAS ASKED FOR MORE.
TSK
TOO MUCH SPACE. NOT ENOUGH SHIPS.
MEANWHILE, WE KEEP PATCHING UP THESE OLD DREAD-NOUGHTS AND HOPING.
HAWKINS, SET A COURSE.
NGUYEN, MONITOR LOCAL COMMS AS WE GET CLOSER.
WE'LL WORK OUT OUR RESPONSE ONCE WE HAVE BETTER INTEL.
IT'S GONNA BE A FIGHT. IT'S ALWAYS A FIGHT.

IT'S NOT A GREAT SITUATION, CAPTAIN.
THE CULT HAS SEIZED THE INDUSTRIAL PROVINCES IN THE NORTHEAST, AND THEY'RE REFUSING TO SEND TRIBUTE.
THINK THEY'LL NEGOTIATE?
MAYBE.
I'M CAPTAIN JUSTIN RAO OF THE I.E.F. DREADNOUGHT INVINCIBLE. WE'RE HERE TO DISCUSS--
NO.
THERE WILL BE NO DISCUSSION.
I'M SORRY.

HAWKINS! WE'RE UNDER ATTACK.
PREP THE INVINCIBLE FOR--
SZAT
CHOOM

WHIRRR
OM
HAWKINS!
INVINCIBLE, RESPOND!
GET BACK TO THE TRANSPORT!
THUK
CHAKCHAK
CHAKCHAKCHAK
I'LL COVER--
BOOM
--FUCK!
TAK
TAK
...
TAK

--?
RUMMMVRMUMMARU
--!
THE INVINCIBLE!
WHAT IN HELL IS HAWKINS--
DUNF
DUNF
DUNF
...!

HAWKINS!
YOU ABSOLUTE BEAUT--
--UH.
HAWKINS IS IN MEDICAL. SHE CRACKED HER HEAD OPEN IN THE FIRST SALVO.
BUT, YOU'RE WELCOME.
HOW.
UHM, HIS CELL TOOK DAMAGE AND HE GOT OUT--
WHAT.
YOU PROMISED ME A FEW MORE WEEKS TO LIVE.
DIDN'T FANCY THOSE BASTARDS CUTTING IT SHORT.
NGUYEN, PLEASE ESCORT THE PRISONER BACK TO THE BRIG.
YOU SHOULD GET SOME REST, SIR. YOU DON'T LOOK SO GOOD.
...YEAH.

BRIG
...
DOOR
TAK
DOMHNALL.
I JUST WANTED TO SAY...
HNNH
...THANK YOU.
FOR NOT RUNNING.
FOR SAVING MY SHIP.
DOOR
WELL. I LIKE DEMETRIA, BUT MY SHIP'S ON KALA IX AND THE ONLY WAY BACK TO HER IS ON HERE.
SO.
AND CALL ME DOM.
WHERE'D YOU LEARN TO FLY A DREADNOUGHT, DOM?
SAME PLACE YOU DID.

YOU WERE I.E.F.?
THERE'S NO RECORD--
--THERE'S NO RECORD BECAUSE WE WERE IN THE SKUNKWORKS ON LYRA WHEN IT WAS RAZED.
WE?
ME AND MY SISTER. YOU KNOW HER AS THE ALECTO.
YOU CAN COME IN, IF YOU WANT.
I DON'T THINK THAT'S A GOOD IDEA.
THOSE EXPERIMENTS. THEY WERE BANNED.
THEY WERE--
--HIDDEN IN A BUNKER SO DEEP IT COULD WITHSTAND A DIRECT HIT.
BY THE TIME WE DUG OUT, THE BASE WAS A GHOST TOWN.

...I'M SORRY.
SO, YOU GOING PLANETSIDE, CAPTAIN?
I ASSUME WE'RE STUCK HERE UNTIL DIVISION SHOWS UP.
NO. I...
...I DON'T.
YOU JUST STAY UP IN ORBIT?
HIGH ABOVE THE PEOPLE YOU SUPPOSEDLY SERVE?
IF PRIVATEERS DIDN'T KEEP HITTING TRIBUTE BARGES, I'D HAVE PLENTY OF TIME TO GO PLANETSIDE.
IF THE I.E.F. DIDN'T TAX THE PLANETS DRY TO SEND TRIBUTE TO A CAPITOL THAT HASN'T RESUPPLIED US OR COMMUNICATED WITH US IN OVER 200 YEARS, WE COULD BOTH GO ON PERMANENT VACATION.
EVER FEAR THAT, RAO?
THAT WE'RE ALONE OUT HERE?
NO.
THAT OUR GREAT EMPIRE DIED OFF AND ALL THAT'S LEFT IS OUR SHITTY LITTLE FRONTIER, TOO REMOTE FOR ANYONE TO BOTHER WITH?
WE'RE A THOUSAND LIGHT YEARS FROM THE CAPITOL. THEY'VE FORGOTTEN US, RAO.
NO. WE'LL GET A COMMUNICATION. THERE ARE MORE DREADNOUGHTS COMING.

WE WERE THE NEXT DREADNOUGHTS. DIVISION GAVE UP, AND MADE US.
DIVISION DIDN'T GIVE UP.
ONE CRACKPOT ADMIRAL TOOK MATTERS INTO HIS OWN HANDS.
AND YOU KNOW THAT, DOM, OTHERWISE YOU'D HAVE GONE BACK TO DIVISION.
WHY DON'T YOU GO DOWN AND SEE HOW PEOPLE ACTUALLY LIVE, RAO? THEN ASK ME WHY WE DIDN'T GO BACK TO THE I.E.F.
WHAT DID YOU DO WITH THE MONEY YOU STOLE, DOM?
EVER BEEN TO DEMETRIA'S SOUTHERN ARCHIPELAGO? THERE'S A BAR AT THE TIP OF THE WINDWARD ISLAND.
GREAT PLACE, RIGHT DOWN AT THE END OF THE WORLD. YOU SHOULD GO THERE SOME TIME.
WHERE'S THE MONEY, DOM? YOU DRINK IT?
SIR, WE'RE RECEIVING A CODED MESSAGE FROM DIVISION.

WHAT IS IT?
ARE THEY SENDING US REINFORCEMENTS FOR DEMETRIA?
NO.
IT'S ABOUT THE PRISONER.
WE NEED TO SEND ANOTHER REPORT.
ABOUT WHAT HE DID FOR US--
THEY'VE ORDERED SUMMARY EXECUTION.
TELL THEM--
SCARLET PROTOCOL, SIR.
NO APPEAL.
UHNH
SET A COURSE FOR KALA IX. HE'D WANT...
THAT SAND-HOLE WHERE WE CAUGHT HIM?
...WE'LL CARRY OUT OUR ORDERS THERE.

--FIND YOU GUILTY OF TWENTY-SIX COUNTS OF PIRACY AGAINST THE I.E.F.'S FRONTIER DIVISION AND HEREBY SENTENCE YOU TO DEATH.
DO YOU HAVE ANY LAST WORDS?

YES.
THANK YOU FOR BRINGING ME BACK HERE.
BACK TO HER.
...
...UNCUFF HIM.
BUT--
NOBODY SHOULD DIE IN CHAINS.
bdip
KLAK

--!
RRRRARRMMMMMMBBBBL

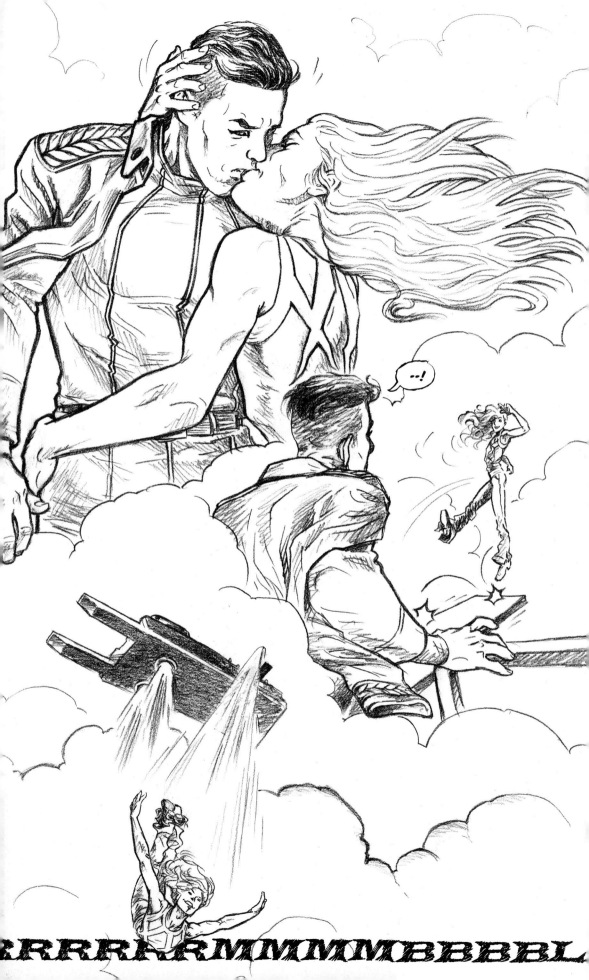

VRRRMMMMMB
DON'T SHOOT.
SST

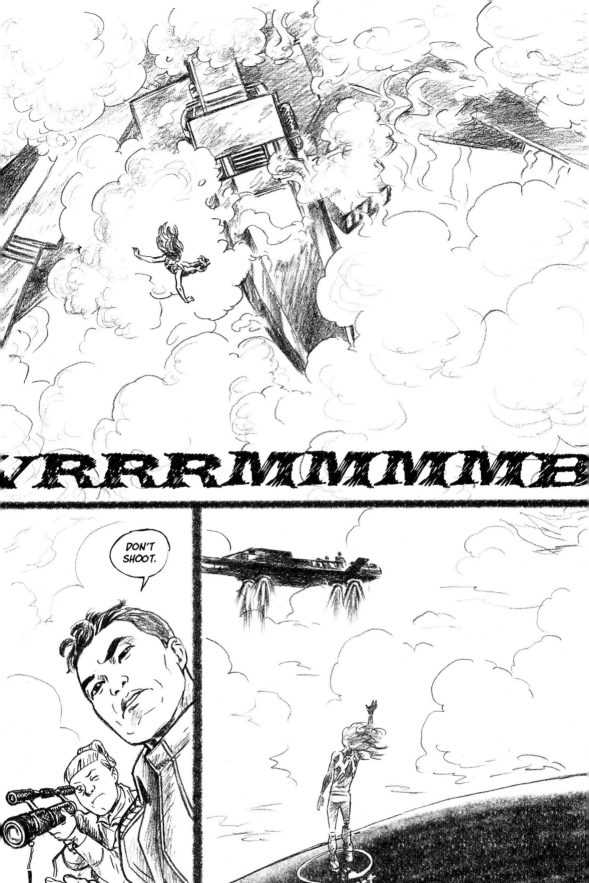

WHAT DO WE TELL DIVISION, CAPTAIN?
THAT WE CARRIED OUT OUR ORDERS.
NOT OUR FAULT HE DIDN'T DIE.
AND WE CAN'T PUNISH HIM TWICE FOR THE SAME CRIME.
BUT SIR--
MATTER CLOSED.
HAWKINS, TAKE FIRST WATCH.
SSSHUNK
...

SET A COURSE BACK TO DEMETRIA.
WE'LL SEE HOW MUCH OF THAT MESS WE CAN UNTANGLE BEFORE BACKUP ARRIVES.
AYE-AYE, LIEUTENANT.

HAWKINS.
CAPTAIN?!
I'VE...
...DECIDED TO TAKE MY ACCUMULATED LEAVE.
YOU'LL BE ACTING CAPTAIN WHILE I'M PLANET-SIDE.
I'LL LET YOU KNOW IF I DIG UP ANY LOCAL INTEL.
SHHUNK
HE NEVER GOES OFF-SHIP.
DOES THE CAPTAIN EVEN OWN CIVILIAN CLOTHES?
I DON'T THINK SO.
IEF
SIR!

UHNH
EXCUSE ME.
HOW DO I GET TO KOH PHANG ISLAND?
HIRE AN OUTRIGGER FROM THE DOCKS--
NO, PLEASE!
KRAK
--!
TSK
NO.
YOU'RE LUCKY WE'RE ONLY TAKING YOUR HOUSE, PAPI.
NEXT TIME, PAY YOUR TAX.
HAA!
THUNK

THERE IS SOMETIMES A **FOREIGNER** AT KOH PHANG.
TALL. LONG HAIR. GOES BY MANY NAMES.
IF YOU SEE HIM, TELL HIM ABOUT THIS.
HE KNOWS HOW TO HELP.
YES, MA'AM!
fwip
SHAA
pff

YOU'RE RIGHT.
THIS IS A GREAT PLACE.
HELLO, SPACE COP. BEEN THINKING ABOUT ME?
YES.
WHAT DO YOU DO WITH THE MONEY YOU STEAL, DOM?

I CAN SHOW YOU.
MMN.
OKAY.
BUT NOT YET.
THE END

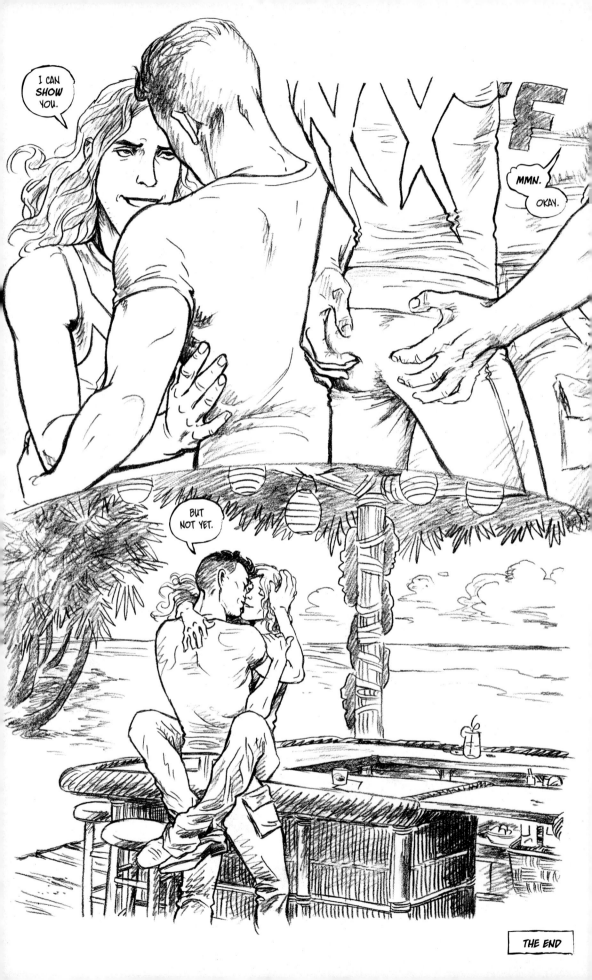

SUPERIOR VENA CAVA
AORTA
PULMONARY ARTERY
PULMONARY VEINS
PULMONARY ARTERY
PULMONARY VEINS
INFERIOR VENA CAVA

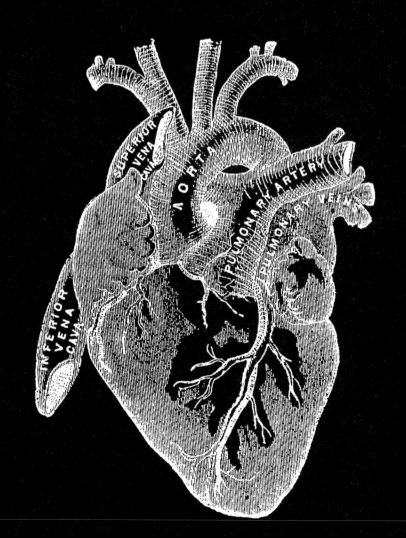

The Last Minute

by Jess Bradley

Hansen stopped to catch her breath and peered up, wiping the sweat from her eyes. They were nearly at the top of the tower and she could see the sickly green glow of the portal above them. She didn't want to look below her to see how far they had climbed because there was no point. They wouldn't be going back down.

"Admiring the view?" Cline's voice was dry and sarcastic. The familiar flare of annoyance his teasing caused was oddly comforting.

He was covering her in case anything down below had seen them climbing the tower. For once, though, luck seemed to be on their side. They'd made it this far undetected. It might not last, and she knew it was stupid to rest. Stupid to assume that they would have a fair shot at this.

"It's fine," Hansen said, and started to climb again.

The tower was a twisted hulk: a half-organic, half-mechanical spire that rose over 300 meters up to the portal. Just looking at it made Hansen feel sick, let alone climbing up it. The matter beneath her feet felt warm even through her heavy boots and it pulsed the same way the portal did, like an egg-sack ready to burst. She had no idea what was actually inside the tower, because there was no visible way in. She suspected that it was just a solid mass, an alien tumor supporting the doorway itself. They were scaling the outside of the tower, using the strange pipes that covered its surface as makeshift steps. That the pipes looked like veins only added to Hansen's nausea.

There was no wind up here, which frightened her more than anything. It was like the portal just absorbed anything rational that she could grasp onto as a scientist.

The glow of portal was getting brighter as she scaled the last couple of meters to the top of the tower. There was a platform of sorts, about 15 meters in circumference, and she walked to the middle and took off her heavy backpack, setting it on the surface.

Cline huffed up behind her and lowered his gun, swiping his face against his sleeve. "Jesus Christ, let's never do that again."

"We won't have to," Hansen muttered as she glanced down at the Earth. You couldn't even call it Earth any more: there was nothing recognisable left. No plants, no trees, no life. Just a rotten, putrid wasteland, alien and repulsive. She turned away before she could let her emotions get the better of her. She had come this far without giving in to them.

Cline watched as she started to carefully unpack the components of the bomb. His gaze slid past her every few seconds, down the way they had come, checking for signs of pursuers who may have seen them from the ground. So far, so good.

"Wouldn't it have been easier just to assemble that thing and then bring it up here?" he asked, glancing over at her with his one good eye.

Hansen forced herself to work slowly. It was tempting to rush, but they only had one chance at this and there was no point in screwing it all up now. They were both going to die anyway.

"I told you before. Once this is assembled it will be highly unstable, and we have to be as close to the portal as possible for it to have the best chance of working. If it had detonated in my pack half-way up this thing, it might only have destroyed the tower, and the portal would still be here and everything we've gone through would have been for nothing."

"Okay, just making conversation," Cline said.

Hansen frowned at him and he shrugged. She still barely knew anything about him; he was in his late thirties and he'd been a professional soldier for most of his adult life. She knew that he'd lost his family during the first wave, but that was about it. He could be caustic and brooding, but he had brought her here despite the odds and hadn't even questioned that he was going to die. Hansen hadn't even really questioned it herself. There had been eight of them at the start of the mission, each accepting that it was all or nothing now. Not wanting to dwell on it too much, she methodically began to assemble the bomb.

Cline paced the platform, looking over but keeping away from the edge. He gave the portal a wide berth. It sat suspended in mid-air just beyond the lip of the platform.

"I feel sick," he said.

"Me too. I think it's the radiation from that thing." Hansen rubbed her temple. A headache was forming.

Cline looked at the portal, at the sickly green light shimmering from it. "I just still can't quite believe this is happening, even after all this time."

Hansen swallowed as she carefully screwed the components of the bomb together. "Me either," she said softly.

The invasion had happened so fast that by the time anyone thought to gather themselves and do something, it was too late. The portal opened above Montana and pulsed for an hour before the horrors started pouring through. Hansen had watched it unfold before the TV stations had gone down, and then she had been participating first-hand in the end of the world. The first couple of weeks had been the worst: the panic and the confusion, the fact that nobody in power had the time to do anything. Hansen had been in Seattle when it started, with her research team, so she had access to secure facilities. Many others weren't so lucky.

In the year since the portal's appearance, it had been a race to find a solution with limited resources and people. The creatures that had come through the portal – they still had no idea where from – ranged vastly in size, ability and biology. A weapon which had a devastating effect on one would have zero effect on another. And it wasn't so much the creatures themselves that were the issue, as the sheer

The tower was a twisted hulk, a half-organic, half-mechanical spire that rose over 300 meters up to the portal. Just looking at it made Hansen feel sick, let alone climbing up it.

number of them. They had swarmed across the planet, ravaging everything in their path.

Those few humans that survived the first wave felt the responsibility of their planet's survival fall on their shoulders. Hansen had been one of them. Simply killing the creatures wasn't really an option. More would just take their place. They had to cut off the source. The portal was the obvious and immediate focus, but there were so many things they still didn't know. Where did it lead? What was it made of? Could they go near it?

The only thing they knew for certain was that before a new wave of creatures spewed out, it emitted larger pulses for an hour. Esquivel was the one who noticed that it pulsed in prime numbers, but by that point it was merely an interesting observation and not anything they could actually use.

The bomb was their last hope of salvaging whatever was left of Earth. Closing the portal was the theory they could all agree on. Maybe closing it would cut the creatures off. Maybe they needed the radiation emitted from the portal to survive. It was all hypotheses even then. And now Hansen and Cline were the only ones left. It was up to her to decide. Cline trusted her judgement and had made it his mission to get her to the end point.

And here they were.

"I always thought it would be a war with nukes that would end the world. Not interdimensional invaders," Cline muttered as he watched her work.

Hansen couldn't help but smile to herself. He was using her term for it rather than saying *from space* like he did when they first met. They hadn't known each other for long, but they had rubbed off on each other in certain ways.

"My money had been on some kind of pandemic," Hansen mused as she tightened the plating on the underside of the bomb.

"What, like zombies?" Cline asked.

"No, more like some mega-strain of flu or Bubonic Plague making a big comeback."

"Makes sense. This –" he waved his gun at the portal – "does not make sense."

Hansen rubbed her temple again. "Maybe it would have if there had been more chances to study it. Time hasn't really been on our side."

"That's one thing you have to give them, I guess. They knew exactly how to disable us: speed and numbers. Overwhelm and subdue."

Hansen nodded in agreement. "*Overwhelm* is the perfect word. They've obviously done this before."

Cline grunted and circled the platform again. "How's that bomb coming? I feel like we're pushing our luck right now. It's never been this quiet."

When they had reached the tower two weeks ago with Stephens and Quinn, the spire had been constantly teeming with a horde of the creatures, climbing up and down and maintaining it, guarding the portal like ants protecting their queen. The four of them had watched from cover a distance away, waiting for the right time to act. The horde had occasionally left the tower, spiralling up into the sky like a murder of crows, and Hansen had timed how long before the creatures returned. The data had shown a pattern, and Stephens and Quinn had been certain they could reach the top of the tower and back with time to spare.

Except that when they had been two-thirds of the way up the tower, the horde had come back, descending on them like a wave. Hansen would always remember how Quinn's scream had just cut off, like someone flipping a switch. She and Cline had remained in cover for the next month, rationing their supplies and making certain that the pattern held before they decided to make their attempt.

"I'm almost there," Hansen said. "Just... talk to me. Give me something to focus on." She always worked better with some other noise in the background: music, TV, talk radio. It had driven her parents and her professors crazy.

"Um, got any vacation plans?"

"You're not funny," Hansen said as she flexed her fingers a few times to stop them from trembling.

Cline kicked at one of the organic pipes on the platform. "Fine, fine. Your surname, that's Swedish, right?"

"No, Danish," Hansen said, relaxing a little. Doing two things at once had always helped her to concentrate. "My dad was from Skagen and met my mom when he came over to the US to teach in New York."

"Are they still in New York?" Cline asked and then threw her an apologetic glance when he realized what he had said. New York had been gone for months. It was easy to forget, sometimes.

"They both died a while back," she said. "Before all of this."

Cline nodded, staring at a point in the distance. Hansen wondered if he was thinking about his family. She often wondered what he thought about. He didn't usually say very much, but he was always listening and watching everything around him. Maybe that's what made him such a good soldier, she thought. He was constantly evaluating the situation for tactical advantage.

She noticed that he did that with people, too. He would say little and then if conflict arose, he would adopt certain mannerisms and speech patterns of the person causing the dispute, diffusing things before they escalated. She had seen him use it when Schafer and Blair had started to butt heads, not long before they were both killed. His quiet facility with people annoyed her in a way; he was so competent and composed, while she felt like she was constantly on the verge of losing it. She was so *tired*. Cline never seemed tired, running on a seemingly endless supply of strength and endurance.

"Do you think this is what they do? Just swarm onto a planet, take it over and then move on?" Cline wondered, poking at the scabby surface of the platform with his gun.

Hansen sat back and grimaced in revulsion when she could feel the tower react, undulating slightly beneath her. "I think so. It's hard to know what they actually want or what they've gained from destroying us. I guess we'll never know now."

"Would you want to know?" Cline asked.

"Yes," Hansen said. "If only so that there was some reason, some *meaning* to put to all of this."

"I don't think they're intelligent. I mean, sure, they're intelligent in the way that they knew exactly what to do to bring us to our knees, but I don't think you could walk up to one and say *Hey, how's it going?* I don't think they have any reason that would make sense to us."

Hansen got back to work fixing the last couple of panels in place. "You know, I think this is the longest conversation we've ever had?"

Cline gave her a wan smile and walked another circuit of the platform. "So this bomb will close the portal?"

"That's the plan. It should stop anything else coming through as well but..." She hesitated. Was it worth giving Cline false hope if she wasn't right?

"But what?" Cline asked.

"Remember when we were in Wolf Creek and Dern threw a grenade at that ground-based horde?" Hansen said.

Cline sighed. That move had cost them most of their supplies. They'd had to abandon camp after the grenade only killed two of the fifty-strong creatures and drew the attention of the rest. It had also cost them Dern, but there was no love lost there for Cline. "Yeah."

"While I was hiding, I watched the horde move away to pursue Dern. But one was left behind. I think it got maimed by the grenade and it couldn't run after the others. The further away they got, the weirder it began to act. It would start veering off to the left and right and eventually it just started to run around in circles."

"So? It was hurt."

Hansen shook her head. "It was, but not too badly from what I could see. I think it needed the horde to function and the further away they got from it, the weaker the signal between them became."

When he turned back to her, his face was softer. He seemed to be struggling to find words. "It's a good theory," he said at last, his voice slightly thick.

Cline's eyes widened a little. "You think it needed the others to survive?"

"It's just a theory," she said quickly. "It could have been anything but... I don't think it was. I think they're a hive mind. I think that's why they could attack so efficiently and quickly. They're always in groups. Which means there's a chance that closing the portal and cutting them off from whatever is on the other side could kill them all."

Cline was silent and Hansen couldn't quite read his face. He turned away and stared out across the shattered landscape.

"Look, I'm probably not the first to think this and there's more than a good chance that I'm wrong. It's... it's all I have."

When he turned back to her, his face was softer. He seemed to be struggling to find words. "It's a good theory," he said at last, his voice slightly thick.

Hansen was a little confused by his reaction; was he annoyed, or did he agree? It was hard to tell with Cline. He very rarely played his hand. She watched him and realized how thin he had become, all lean muscle where he had been stockier at the start of the mission, his brown hair now peppered with grey. He had kept it short the whole time they had been travelling, trimming it with one of the knives sheathed in his belt. He had let his stubble grow in the last week and it softened his face a little, drawing her eyes away from his scar. She thought that maybe he had been handsome once, back when all he had to worry about were bills and how well his kids were doing in school.

Hansen tried not to think about how she must look. She had caught her reflection in what was left of a gas station restroom a few months back and had been frightened by what she had seen. Her dark hair had been greasy and streaked with grey too, pulled back into a ponytail she barely took out. Her olive skin had a tired grey pallor to it and her eyes, framed by dark circles, had looked wild and terrified. That can't be me, she had thought but it was and she had run from the mirror and hadn't looked in one since.

She pulled her attention back to the bomb and finished assembling it. Everything was still eerily quiet. The portal sent out its sickly glow beside them.

The last panel clicked into place. Hansen put down her tools. "Okay. I think we're set," she said.

This was it. Everything they had worked for in the last year had led to this moment. The trek from Seattle to Montana, watching the others die, switching off parts of themselves to be able to keep going and not give up; everything had always pointed to *this* end game. Now that the moment was here, Hansen was finally able to admit to herself that she was terrified. She had made her peace with dying a while ago, but it was everything she didn't know that scared her. Would the bomb work? Were there enough people left in the world to take it back if it did? Would it hurt when she died?

To her knowledge, there had been no other attempts to end the invasion. Communications had been shut down so rapidly, what was left of her department had just decided to build what they could with the materials at their disposal and go for it. For all they knew, she and Cline were the last ones left to do anything. That knowledge weighed down on her.

"This could all be for something or all be for nothing," she muttered to herself.

Cline clenched his jaw. "We have to hope it's for something. I can't... I can't die and think it was all for nothing."

Hansen stood up and stepped as close to the edge of the platform as she dared. The silence around them made her stomach churn; it wasn't natural. "We should do this now," she said. "A swarm could come back at any time."

She suddenly felt for him, this quiet, stoic soldier, lost for words at the end of the world. She felt for all of them, a sharp pang in her heart, the ghosts and the dead and the gone.

Cline set his gun down. "Okay," he said and she could hear the fear in his voice too.

"You don't have to do this. You could climb back down and get as far away as you can," Hansen said. "The bomb might not reach as far as we think, you could get away – "

"I'm not *leaving you* to do this on your own," Cline said; the anger in his voice surprised her. "You really think I'd help you get all the way here and then just *leave*?"

Hansen shook her head, feeling bad that she'd insulted him. "No," she said quietly. "I'm sorry."

Cline sighed. "Me too. It's... this is messed up," he said miserably.

Hansen pushed down the sob that was making its way up her throat. She wasn't going to let herself fall apart now. "It is. But there's a chance we could be making a big difference to everything." She managed a smile.

"Hansen, I have to tell you something..." Cline began. He glanced down at his combat boots and swallowed.

She suddenly felt for him, this quiet, stoic soldier, lost for words at the end of the world. She felt for all of them, a sharp pang in her heart, the ghosts and the dead and the gone. "It's been a honor working with you too, Cline," she said, smiling.

"...I love you."

Hansen stared at him for a moment, because of all the things she had expected him to say, that wasn't any of them. "You... *what?*"

"I'm in love with you," he said. There was nothing but complete, raw honesty on his face.

Hansen stared at him again. She rolled the statement around in her head but it still made no sense. "What are you talking about? How can you be in love with me?"

"Because I just am," he said, simply. He wasn't embarrassed or awkward, just calm. She had never seen him this calm before. "I just wanted to tell you before we..." he waved his hand toward the portal.

Hansen floundered. What was she supposed to *do* with this information? They were both about to die attempting to save what was left of the Earth from a hostile alien invasion and Cline goes and drops *this* into her lap. They had been working side by side for a year, sure, but he had never given any indication that he felt any way towards her other than a soldier doing his job.

"Why would you tell me this now?" she said, her voice slightly louder than she'd intended it to be.

"I just wanted you to know," Cline said, his strong shoulders slumping in defeat.

The surreality of their situation struck Hansen again. She was finding it hard to think straight between her headache from the portal radiation and what Cline was talking about. He had no *right* to do this. Not *now*. Anger flared in her chest. "Look, I know it's maybe the end of the world and we're about to die but I'm not going to do anything with you just for the sake of it –"

"Oh God, no!" Cline cried and he recoiled. "No! That's not what I want. That's not what I mean by this." He closed his eye and gathered himself. "I've fallen in love with you, that's all."

"That's all?" Hansen repeated. She pointed at the bomb, the tower and the portal in succession. "Look where we are and what we're doing!"

Cline stared down at his hands. "Hansen..."

"I don't have feelings for you," Hansen said. She wasn't sure if she was angry at Cline for confessing to her or sad for him, but she had to tell him the truth.

Cline looked up at her. "I know." He was so damn *calm*. Hansen always hated how calm he was. How he could settle their fractious, motley group of scientists, soldiers and refugees by the force of his quiet competence. She'd secretly always wanted to see him lose his cool, see him riled up, so *she* could be the calm one. And here he is baring his damn heart to her and he's still so collected.

Hansen throws up her hands. "Then why tell me?"

Cline chewed on his lip. It made him look so young, so *unsure*, and Hansen was again reminded of the man he must have been before... before everything went to shit. "When my family died, that was it for me," he said. He blinked rapidly and squinted at the portal. "I shut myself down. My brain switched over to automatic pilot and I just did what I was told. I was there but I *wasn't*, not inside. Then I got assigned to your team. I thought it was doomed to fail from the start. I mean, why would anything work against those things? I was going to do my best, but... I didn't hold out much hope for us. I knew Blair and Schafer were going to be trouble and Dern was pretty far gone by the time we got out of Seattle. Stephens and Quinn only came with us because we were the best bet at the time, but they would have left in a second if something better came along."

He absently rubbed at the scar that ran from his forehead to his left cheekbone. His eyelid was fused shut, just a part of the twisted shiny pink flesh and skin on that side of his face. She had never asked him how it had happened.

"You were different. When we started out, you had this determination that the others didn't have and I remember thinking, *She'll lose that. It won't last*. I waited and watched and if anything, whatever happened to us, your determination just *grew*. I started to admire you. It was like the further we got, the more selfless you became, even when the others died. Schafer ran away to save his own skin and he's probably dead now, Blair tried to sabotage the mission and I..." he cleared his throat. "You know what I had to do."

Hansen nodded dumbly. Blair had snapped and tried to kill everyone. Cline had taken no pride in his decision and she knew he didn't live with it lightly.

"At any point you could have stopped or given up, but you didn't. All this time, all you've wanted to do was save the world," Cline said.

"And that was enough for you?" Hansen asked.

Cline gave a tired little nod of his head. All that was commanding and severe had drained out of his posture, and he just stood there, a man who had lost everything that meant anything to him.

"But you don't even *know* me," she said desperately. "You don't know my favorite color or my favorite book or *anything*."

"I know, but it doesn't change how I feel."

The portal suddenly started to pulse. Two flashes. Three flashes. Five. A new wave was getting ready to come through. They both stared at it and the clock started to tick faster.

"Saved by the bell," Cline said wryly.

Hansen was exhausted. She barely had anything left to give at this point; the last year had taken everything out of her. Their food and water had run out yesterday. The climb up the tower had been achieved on pure adrenaline and now that the bomb was ready to be activated, she was overcome by a bone-deep tiredness. She watched the portal pulse and counted the undulations: *Seven*.

"Hansen?" Cline said softly.

Hansen turned back to him. Her body felt heavy. "I'm so tired," she muttered.

Cline made a motion to reach out for her hand but stopped. "I'm sorry. I'm sorry I laid this on you now, but I've been a coward about so many things in my life and I didn't want to be a coward about this."

"I don't love you back. I can't even pretend that had all of this not happened and we knew each other better, there might have been a chance," she said, meeting his eye.

"I'm not asking for that," Cline said. "When we started out on this mission, I didn't think it would work. I didn't care, I didn't care about anything but then as we got closer and every-one else started to fall apart, you didn't. And I just..." He shrugged helplessly. "You kept me going. You made me realize that there was meaning to what we were doing. That we weren't doing this for ourselves." He let out a breath and she finally saw the same exhaustion in him that she was feeling.

"You were differ-ent. When we started out, you had this determi-nation that the others didn't have and I remember thinking, She'll lose that. It won't last."

The portal continued to pulse steadily beside them. *Eleven*.

Hansen could feel herself start to crumble. She'd held on for so long, not letting fear and despair overtake her, focussed on just getting here and doing what they needed to do and now it was starting to unwind. It was too much to know that he felt this way when all she had done was what she thought she had to, holding everyone at arm's length because what good would it have done to form attachments when this was always how it was going to end?

All this time she thought she had been alone, and she hadn't been. Being with her had meant something to him; she had been holding herself together so she wouldn't disappoint him and he had been carrying on because of her. Suddenly, all she could feel was regret. Regret for not having made more of an effort to get to know him. She knew she could never love him in the same way he loved her, but they could have been friends. It seemed like such a waste, and it had never even crossed her mind.

"I'm sorry," she said. "I wish this could be different."

Cline smiled, crooked and easy. He must have been quite a charmer once, she thought. "I don't. After everything that's happened, I never thought I'd ever feel anything but anger and grief again. But I was wrong. I have you to thank for that."

It was overwhelming to think that she had given him something so big without even realizing it. Hansen couldn't take that away from him. "You're welcome."

Cline laughed and it was such a good sound, honest and... happy. There hadn't been any happiness for either of them in a long time. "This is going to work. We're going to save the world."

Hansen couldn't help but smile. "We are." The smile slipped from her face as she glanced over Cline's shoulder. There was a dark cloud on the horizon. "Shit."

Cline turned around and cursed under his breath. It was a swarm. A big one. "Okay, we need to move fast; we've got maybe five minutes at the rate they're moving."

Hansen panicked and stumbled as she went to pick up the bomb. This was it. She put her hands on her knees and took a deep breath. She felt a hand on her shoulder and Cline was there beside her.

"It's all right," he said softly. "Everything's going to be all right."

"I'm so scared," she said. She wanted to cry but didn't think she physically had it in her.

Cline swallowed. "Me too."

They both moved at the same time and held each other tightly. The warmth of his arms around her was almost a relief. She savored this last little vestige of human contact. She hadn't been held like this in a long time. Hansen closed her eyes and muttered into Cline's shoulder.

"What?" he asked, pulling back to look at her.

"Yellow and *To Kill A Mockingbird*."

Cline looked confused for a second and then he laughed again. "Green and *War Of The Worlds*, although given the current situation that might have changed."

Hansen laughed with him and her fear subsided a little. "I don't even know your first name," she said.

"Daniel. Danny."

"Naomi."

They both stood together and Hansen held the bomb, turning to the portal. It was pulsing rapidly now.

"How long before that thing blows when it's activated?" Cline asked.

"Around three seconds."

Cline let out a shaky breath. "I guess we need

Cline laughed and it was such a good sound, honest and happy. There hadn't been any happiness for either of them in a long time. "We're going to save the world."

to get as close to the portal as possible." He scanned the horizon. The cloud was growing bigger and darker.

They stepped as near to the edge of the tower as they could. Hansen stared at the portal, now less than two feet in front of her. She couldn't see anything through the green haze it sent out and she wondered for the millionth time what lay beyond. Given the horrors that had come out of it, she thought it must be as close to Hell as anything could be.

When she glanced at Cline again, he looked terrified. His one good eye was welling up with tears. She felt as afraid as he did, but he had given her something too, right at the end when she thought there was nothing left. She tucked the bomb under her right arm, her thumb resting next to the activation switch and took his hand with her left. Cline looked down at her hand in his, and then up at her.

"I'm glad I made it here with you. With anyone else, it would've been meaningless," she said, and as the words left her, she knew it was true.

Cline brought her hand to his lips and gave it a small, quick kiss before lowering it again, still holding onto it tightly. "Thank you, Naomi."

"Ready?" she asked.

Cline nodded and they both turned to face the portal, their backs to the rapidly darkening sky. "Ready."

Hansen wasn't scared any more. If this worked, they were giving the world back to whoever was left and good things could happen again. That was the only thought in her mind now. All of the what-ifs and theories were kicked aside and a seed of hope was suddenly growing before her into a vast forest where only a void had existed before.

"This is going to work," she said.

Still holding Cline's hand, Hansen activated the bomb.

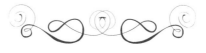

"Olivia Lies, Pierced" • by Margaret Trauth • with help from Nick Brienza • ©2017
Walk with me, Soror Featherstone.
Tell me why you and Frater Konstanținscu shut down the Academy's water tower last night.
Would you believe, um, a cultural appreciation exchange that got out of hand?
...maybe.
Tell me more.
Frater Sapientes Taren Burrhus, PH.L, D.S. 3
Specialties: topology, pyrokinetic data decompression.
Current role: student advisor.
Olivia Featherstone
Soror Aspirans, Second Class
Current role: in trouble. Again.
STAISBRIDGE ACADEMY of DIPLOMACY, HONSMOT ORBITAL // LAST NIGHT
Choose your weapon, o Prince.
I still can't decide if this is the best idea you've ever had, or your worst.
student-grade force rapier
passes through flesh, interacts with fields
clashes dramatically on impact
100% safe!
Aww, c'mon, K. This is gonna be the most badass thing we do all semester.
And you showed up in a Mutinous Princess Iolanda costume! You are so into this.
I, uh, brought a costume for you, too, if you—
EN GARDE!
Klaudoscu Accha Lăzares Belesich Konstanținscu, Eighth Heir of Vauteil
Frater Aspirans, Third Class
("Baron K" to his friends)
Current role: bemused offworlder

Holy buttsauce, did she just... why is Iolanda a *tree* now, what the... This is based on *your actual history*?
SEVEN WEEKS AGO
Well. Mostly. Kinda. Look, it's for *kids*, okay? I didn't say it
dude stop apologizing this is *great*
K. insisted that I'd insulted "the rich culture of his homeworld" and the only thing for it was a formal duel. Under as many full moons as possible.
That's quite a reaction.
Yeah! I was just ribbing him about watching that goofy pre-Contact vidshow of his all the time!
frrzztt
FOUR WEEKS AGO
No, that's Iolanda's friend Coelestine, the one with the pet quillfett, remember?
Oh yeah. That creepy, creepy quillfett.
I mean that was also after he called me an emotionless devotee of the Codex...
and that was after I hacked his dining profile so all he had to eat for a week was blusterberry cake
You're getting predictable, Liv. Try again.
For *real* this time.
...which I think was in revenge for when he gave me
That will suffice, Soror Featherstone. I see you and our noble friend still have *quite* the healthy relationship.

anyway, that morning he'd called me a pile of mugnog droppings for making fun of *Mutinous Princess Iolanda* and told me to meet him up there that night, *or else*.
Mm-*hmm*.
YESTERDAY MORNING
Hey, pinknose!
Hey, K, wait up.
I hear it's your birthday. Gotcha something,
Oh geeze, you didn't need to, it's not even for a week yet...
what *is* this?
Clip it to your blouse and find out!
arm field strength
high
Ooooh. Pretty!
click! VVVVVVVVVV
I was getting a little melancholy this morning but this makes me feel a lot less homesi—

ahem
Tonight, atop the water tower, we meet on the field of honor.
"By blade...
"...by hope, by love, by steel, we prove our power now.
"For the Souls of the Stars!"*
uh Liv, um, you know the tower's off-limits right
Yup!
we are gonna be in so much trouble if they catch us
Yyyup!
like, who'd have thought he'd care so much about this goofy Iolanda kids' show?
Well. "There is nothing so small it can't be blown out of proportion."**
* From Mutinous Princess Iolanda,

We fought on top of the water tower for, oh, half an hour. I kinda wish we hadn't disabled the security eyes beforehand, now. I bet we looked **amazing**.
You'll be happy to know you missed a couple of them, then. I'm looking forward to hearing what your close-combat instructors thought of it.
uh-oh
Fizz buckles, Olivia! Are you alright?
I'm, uh, fine? Huh. It's not coming back on.
I think we're done here? We should get your arm fixed tomorrow?
"Failure is not fatal; it is the courage to continue that counts."*
*ibid, episodes 4, 9, 13, and 14.
Well. If you're gonna quote Iolanda's final words at me...
None of the eyes you missed saw who shut down the field, though.
Well. Um...

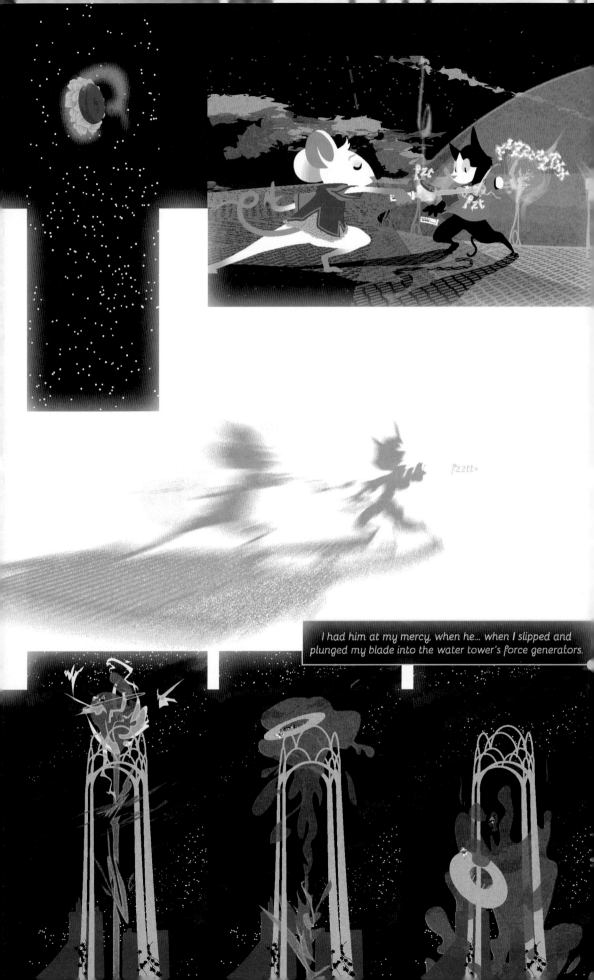

I had him at my mercy, when he... when I slipped and plunged my blade into the water tower's force generators.

SMOOCH
I didn't—
mmm
...then, well, Tranquility Enhancement caught up with us, we spent the night in separate cells, maintenance helped reboot my arm, and now here I am about to find out if I'm gonna be a getting on a ship back to New Chakonia for the rest of my life, I guess...

I'm *impressed*, Cadet Fourth Class Featherstone. Your story matches up with Frater K's *much* better than the last three times we had this sort of chat.
I would, however, advise you to consider the long-term consequences of who you're choosing to take the fall for your combined antics. *Anything is easier to take apart than to put together.**
Uhhh... thank you, Frater Burrhus.
Feel the rush of power the wind of defeat the melancholy for a world that never was...‡
* Vexalyne Edification Codex, 10th Ed. 14.107:2
‡ Mutinous Princess Iolanda, title theme.
You're welcome. Now then. You'll be spending an hour of every day with the grounds crew, until they and myself both feel you've covered for the mess you made.
And, on a more personal note...
Yes, Frater?
I suggest that you and that boy work out the *precise* shape of your relationship in less... *dramatic* ways.
While we still have an *Academy* for you two to *flirt* in.
What was he whispering before he left?
Oh, nothing, the... the usual threats of expulsion if we don't end the term near the head of the class.
Pfff. As if we were planning on doing anything differently than the *last* three semesters.
secret handshake!
Maybe we should.
What was that?
Nothing.
Nothing at all.

VI
THE LOVERS.

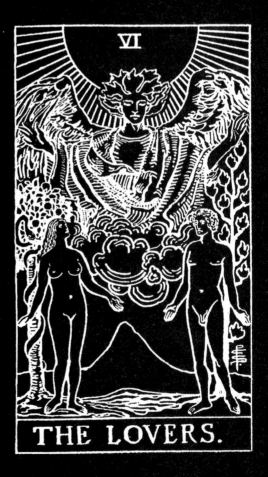

Trungles Alex de Campi

Treasured

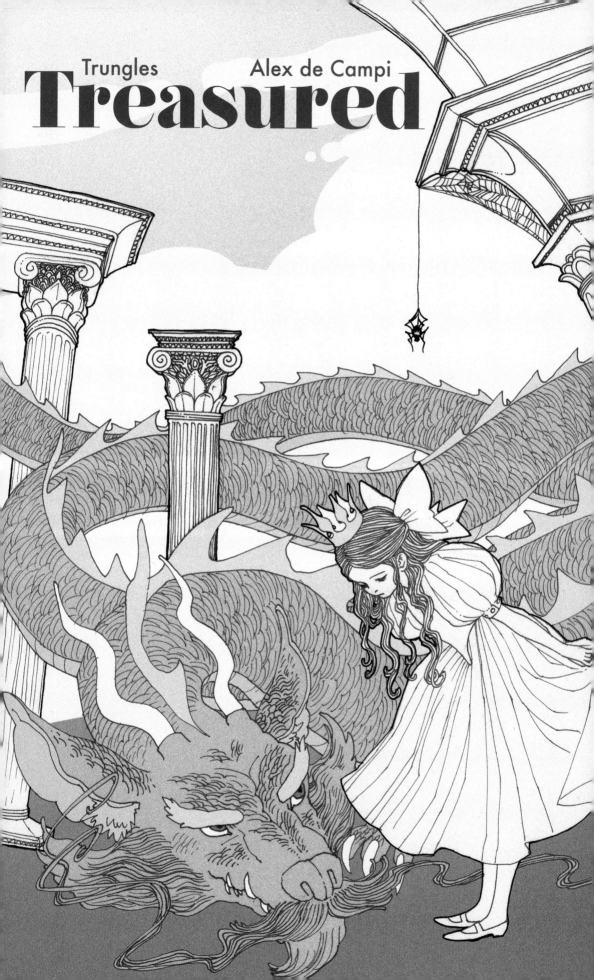

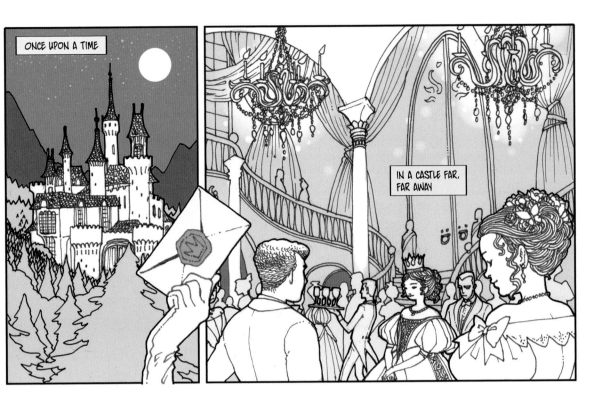

ONCE UPON A TIME

IN A CASTLE FAR, FAR AWAY

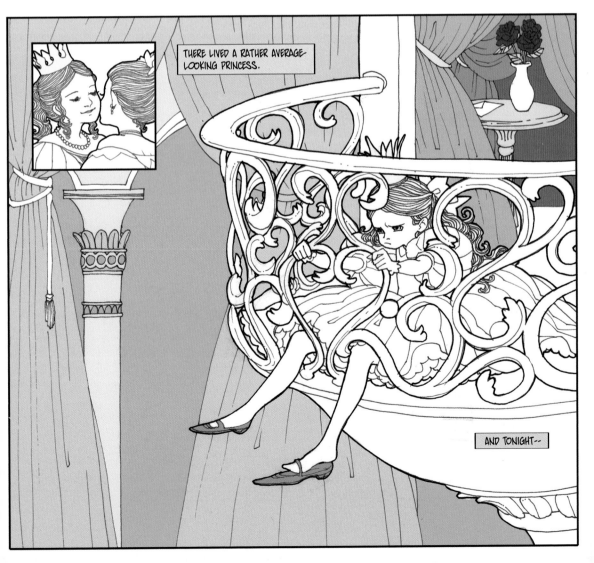

THERE LIVED A RATHER AVERAGE-LOOKING PRINCESS.

AND TONIGHT--

--TONIGHT SHE WOULD BE PRESENTED TO **SOCIETY**.
AND SHE WAS VERY
VERY
VERY
AWFULLY
DISPLEASED ABOUT THIS.

KLAK
YOUNG LADY!
GET DOWN HERE AT ONCE!
HMPH!
GASP!

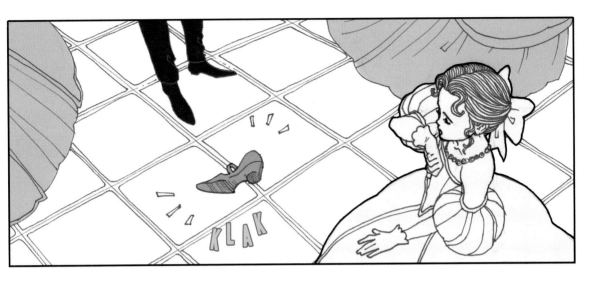

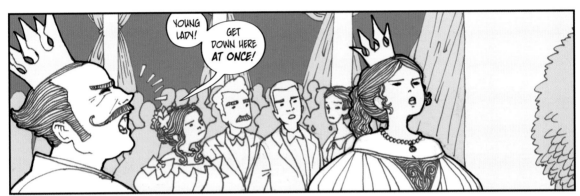

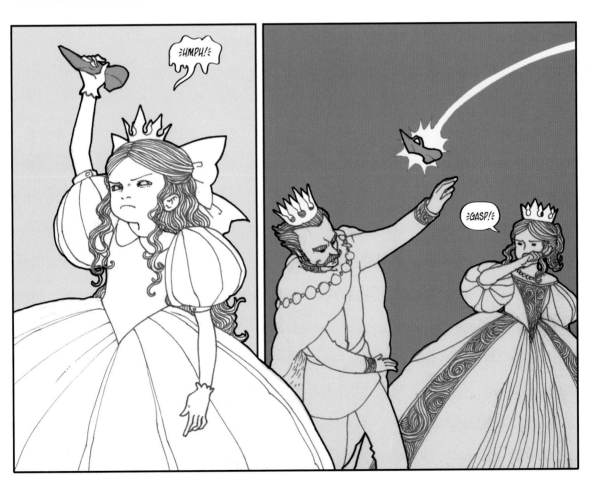

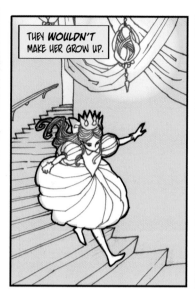

THEY **WOULDN'T** MAKE HER GROW UP.

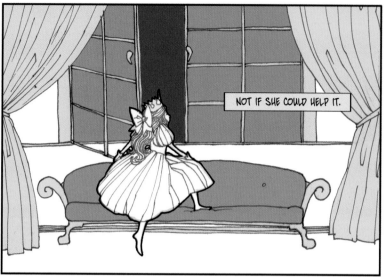

NOT IF SHE COULD HELP IT.

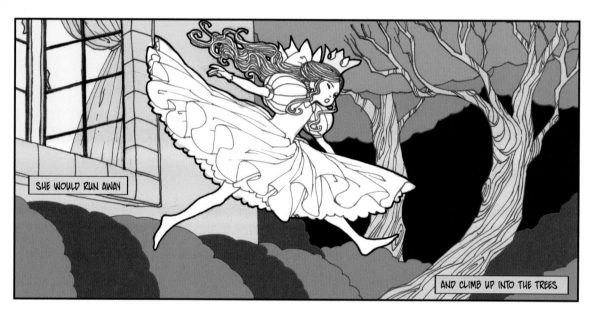

SHE WOULD RUN AWAY

AND CLIMB UP INTO THE TREES

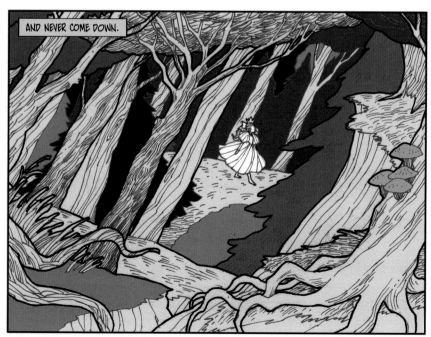

AND NEVER COME DOWN.

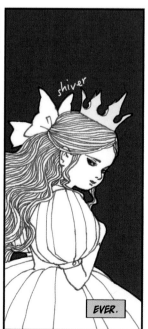

shiver

EVER.

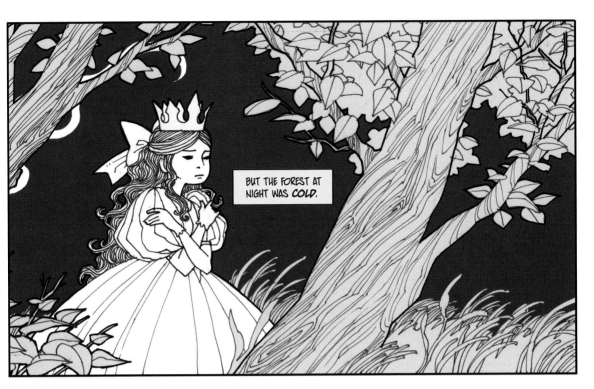

BUT THE FOREST AT NIGHT WAS *COLD*.

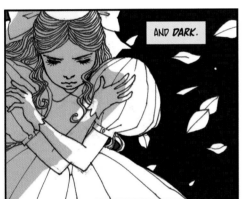

AND *DARK*.

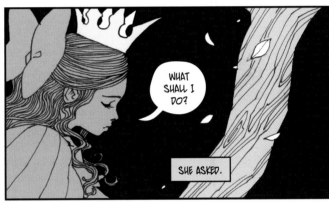

WHAT SHALL I DO?

SHE ASKED.

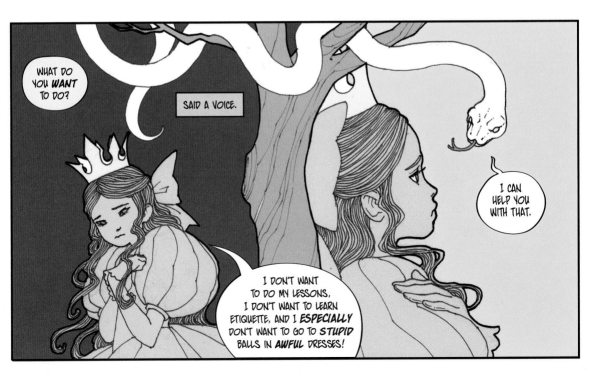

WHAT DO YOU *WANT* TO DO?

SAID A VOICE.

I CAN HELP YOU WITH THAT.

I DON'T WANT TO DO MY LESSONS, I DON'T WANT TO LEARN ETIQUETTE, AND I *ESPECIALLY* DON'T WANT TO GO TO *STUPID* BALLS IN *AWFUL* DRESSES!

JUST GIVE ME A KISS.
FOR JUST AS YOU ARE A PRINCESS WITH THE SOUL OF A BIRD...
...I AM A SERPENT WITH THE HEART OF A DRAGON.
IT COULDN'T BE WORSE THAN THE HON. ALGERNON PETTIGREW
WHO TRIED TO SMOOCH HER IN THE LIBRARY AFTER LATIN.
ALGERNON HAD BEEN CLAMMY WITH SWEAT, AND SMELLED OF MOULDY CRACKERS.
THE SNAKE WAS DRY, AND SMELLED FAINTLY OF STRANGE METALS.
NOW I AM MIGHTY AGAIN.

AND YOU ARE MY
TREASURE

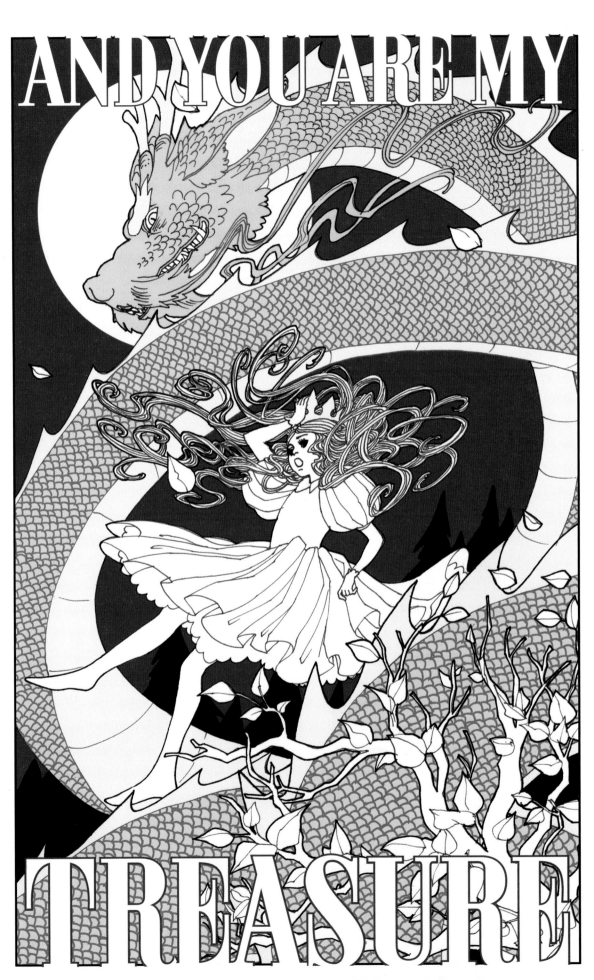

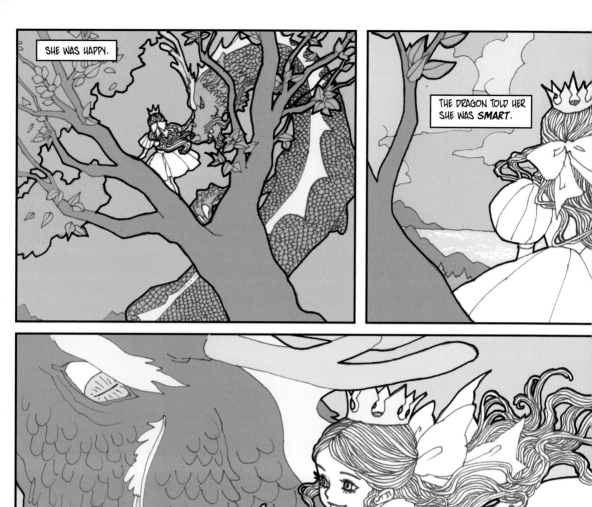

SHE WAS HAPPY.

THE DRAGON TOLD HER SHE WAS **SMART**.

AND **BEAUTIFUL** BEYOND COMPARE.

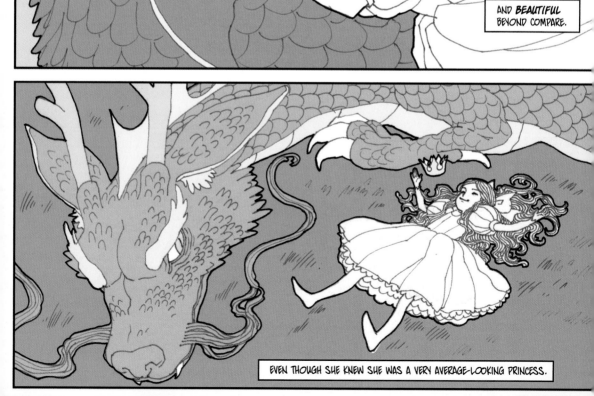

EVEN THOUGH SHE KNEW SHE WAS A VERY AVERAGE-LOOKING PRINCESS.

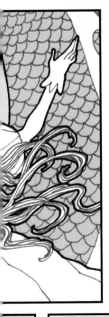

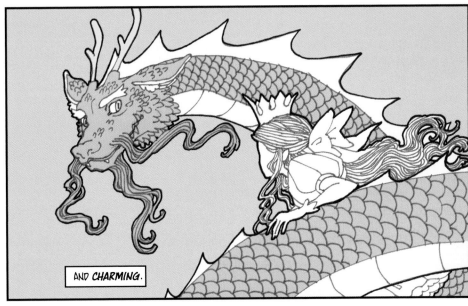

AND **CHARMING**.

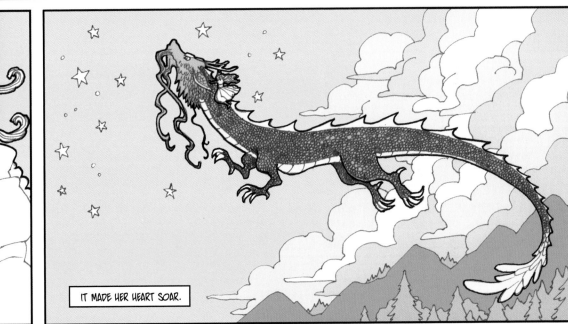

IT MADE HER HEART SOAR.

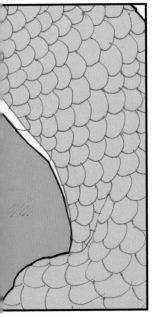

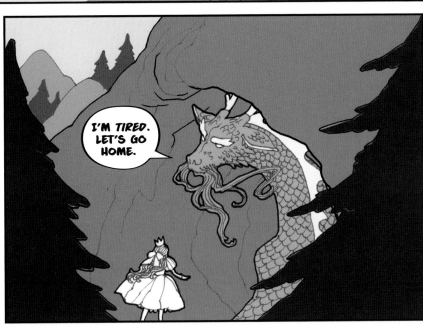

I'M *TIRED*. LET'S *GO* HOME.

BEING TREASURE WASN'T ALL IT WAS CRACKED UP TO BE.
TIME PASSED.
IN LOVING MEMO
THE KINGDOM DECLARED HER DEAD.
PANIC at the PALACE
ISSING PRINCESS
Unicorn corpses found scattered throughout Kingdom. Continued on B2.
NO KNIGHTS CAME.

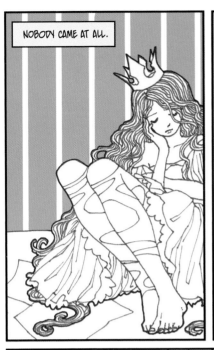

NOBODY CAME AT ALL.

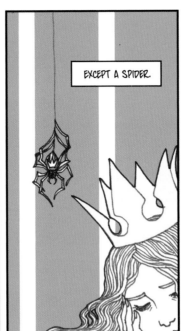

EXCEPT A SPIDER.

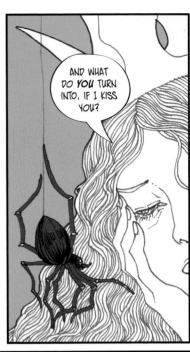

AND WHAT DO *YOU* TURN INTO, IF I KISS YOU?

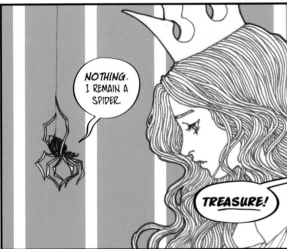

NOTHING. I REMAIN A SPIDER.

TREASURE!

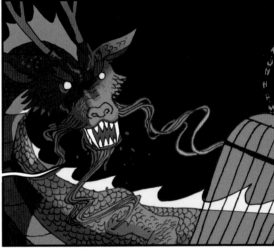

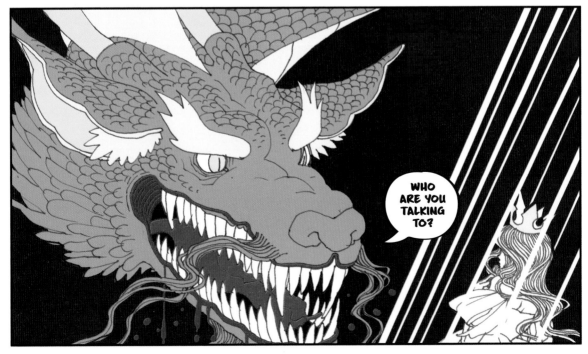

WHO ARE YOU TALKING TO?

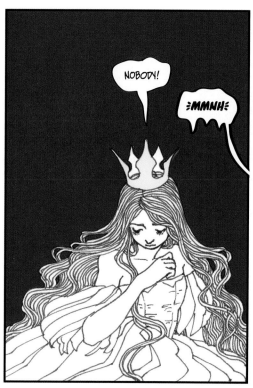

NOBODY!

≥MMNH≤

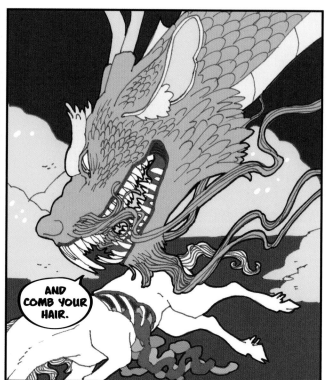

AND COMB YOUR HAIR.

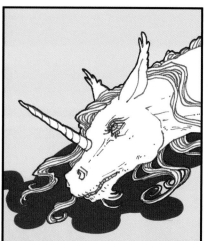

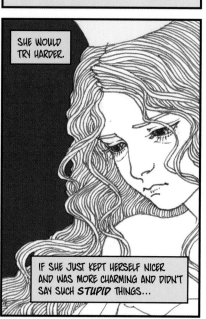

SHE WOULD TRY HARDER.

IF SHE JUST KEPT HERSELF NICER AND WAS MORE CHARMING AND DIDN'T SAY SUCH *STUPID* THINGS...

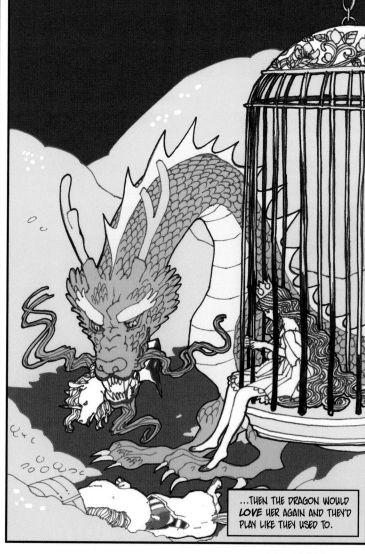

...THEN THE DRAGON WOULD *LOVE* HER AGAIN AND THEY'D PLAY LIKE THEY USED TO.

MAYBE EVEN GO OUT INTO THE SUN AGAIN.
OR PERHAPS A KNIGHT WOULD COME.
BUT APPARENTLY ONLY *BEAUTIFUL* PRINCESSES WERE RESCUED.
AND SHE WAS JUST AVERAGE.
IT'S NOT *THAT* BAD.
HE DOESN'T HIT HER.
IF SHE JUST *BEHAVES*--

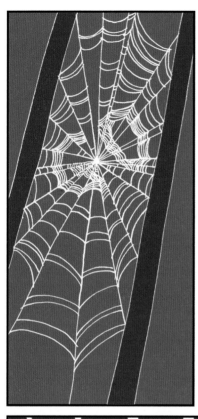

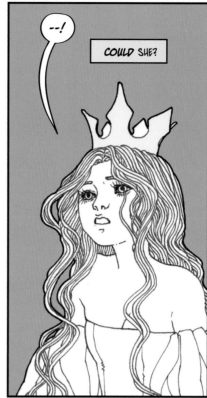

--!

COULD SHE?

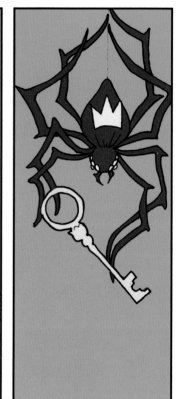

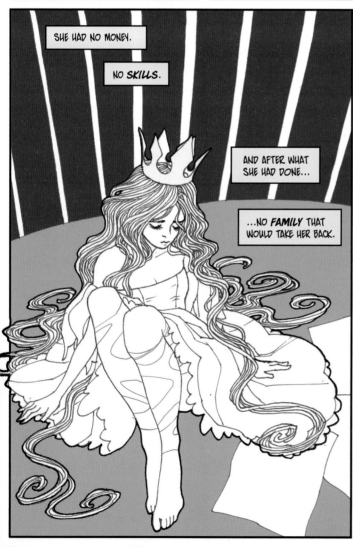

SHE HAD NO MONEY.

NO SKILLS.

AND AFTER WHAT SHE HAD DONE...

...NO FAMILY THAT WOULD TAKE HER BACK.

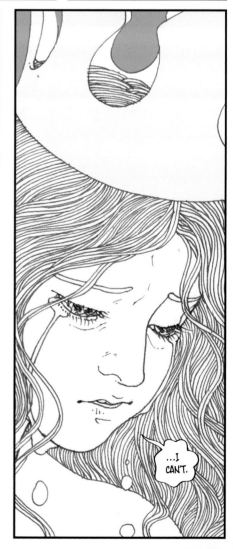

...I CAN'T.

sff
ARE YOU RESCUING ME?
NO.
I AM JUST A SPIDER.
YOU HAVE TO RESCUE YOURSELF.
tnk
I CAN'T.
HE'LL-
blink

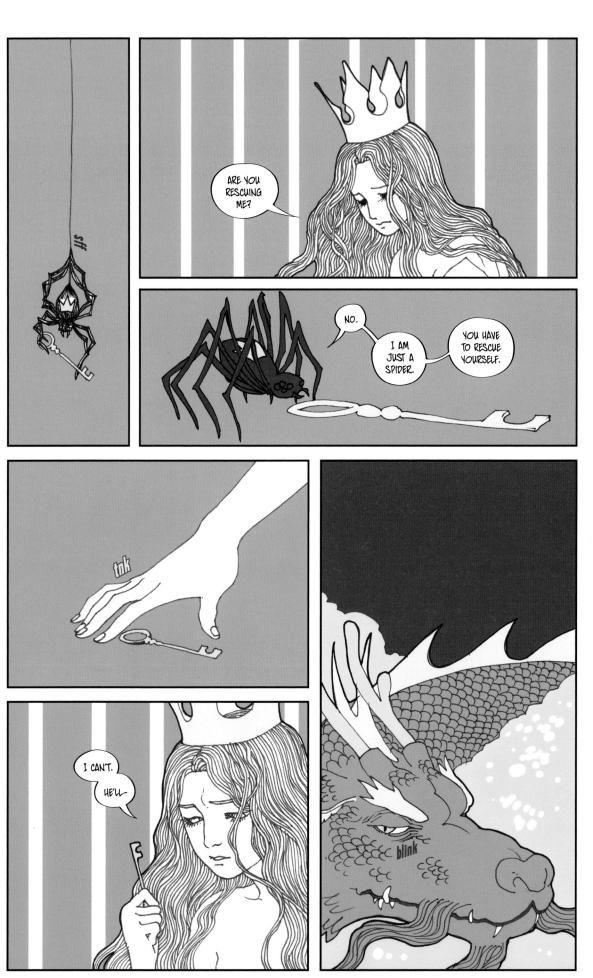

WHAT IS THIS?!
CHANK
AAH!
MINE.
PLEASE! PLEASE, I'M SORRY.
I'M SORR-
SKRASH

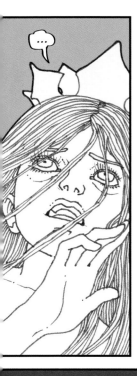

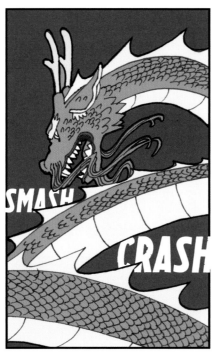

SMASH

CRASH

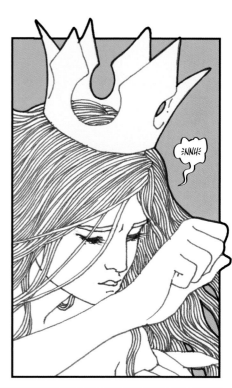

=NNH=

I WAS GOING TO TAKE YOU OUTSIDE TOMORROW.

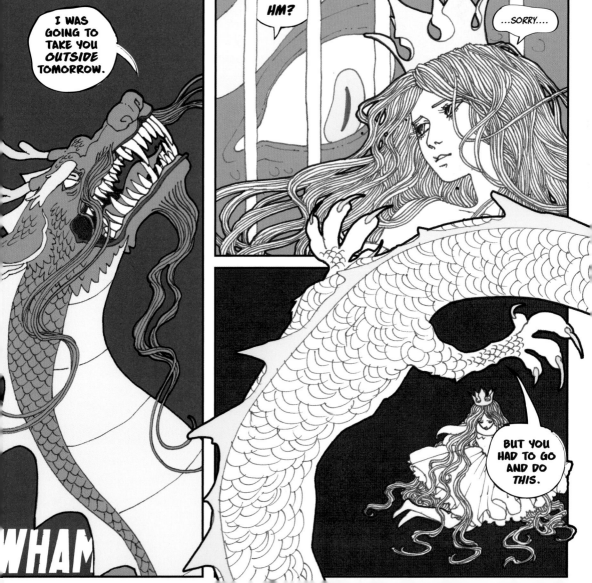

HM?

...SORRY....

BUT YOU HAD TO GO AND DO THIS.

WHAM

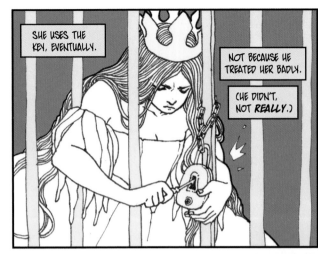

SHE USES THE KEY, EVENTUALLY.

NOT BECAUSE HE TREATED HER BADLY.

(HE DIDN'T, NOT *REALLY*.)

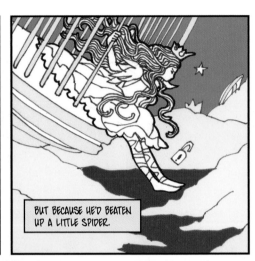

BUT BECAUSE HE'D BEATEN UP A LITTLE SPIDER.

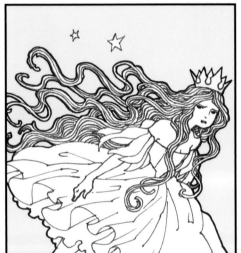

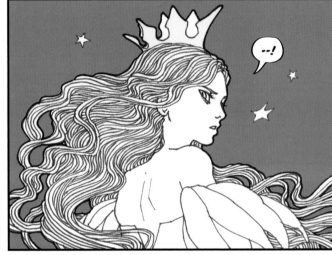

--!

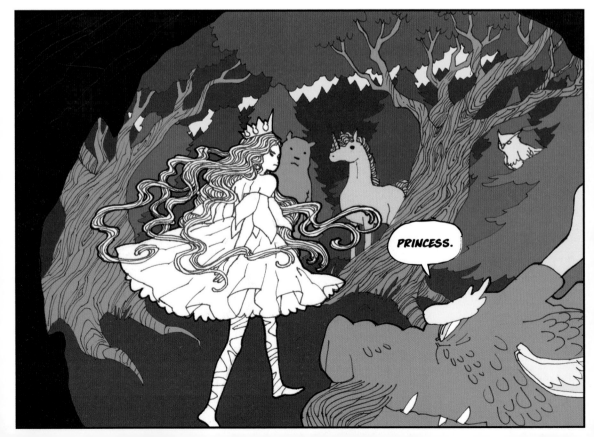

PRINCESS.

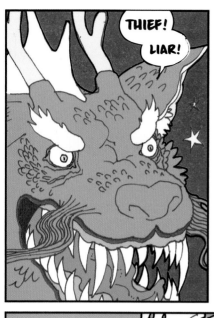

THIEF!
LIAR!

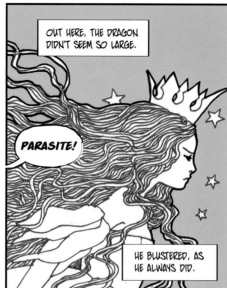

OUT HERE, THE DRAGON DIDN'T SEEM SO LARGE.

PARASITE!

HE BLUSTERED, AS HE ALWAYS DID.

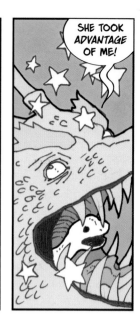

SHE TOOK ADVANTAGE OF ME!

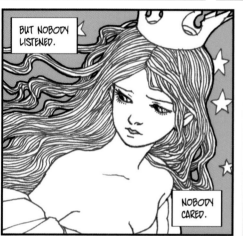

BUT NOBODY LISTENED.

NOBODY CARED.

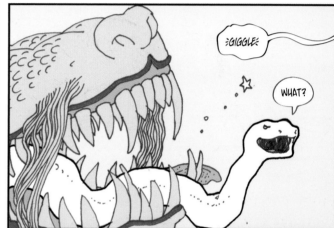

≶GIGGLE≷

WHAT?

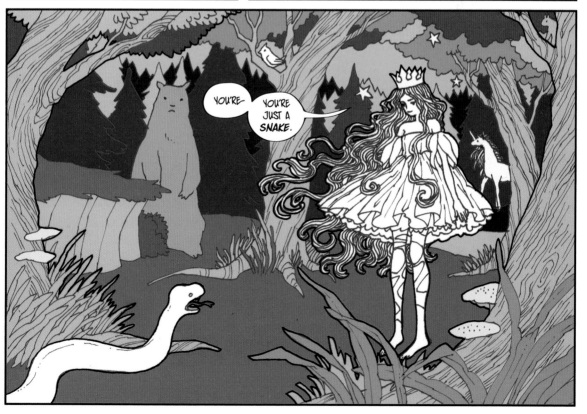

YOU'RE— YOU'RE JUST A SNAKE.

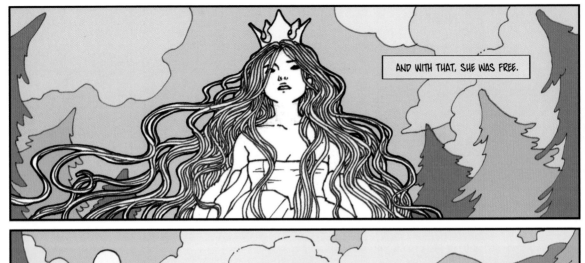

AND WITH THAT, SHE WAS FREE.

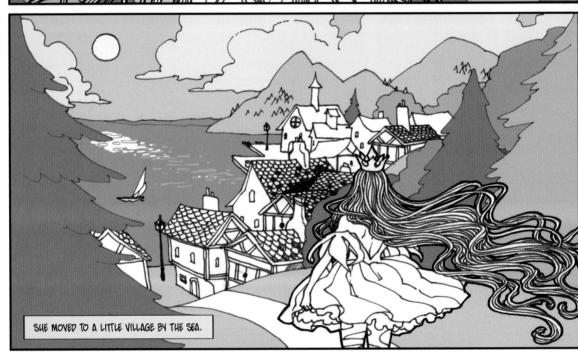

SHE MOVED TO A LITTLE VILLAGE BY THE SEA.

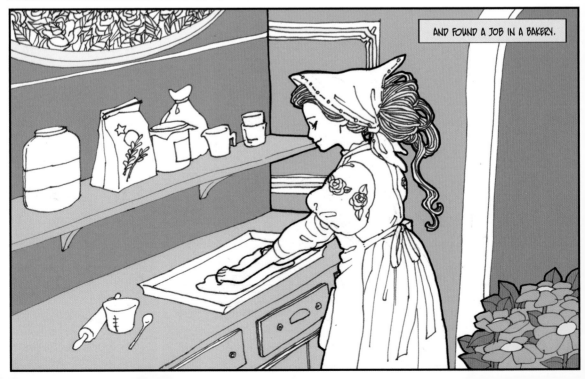

AND FOUND A JOB IN A BAKERY.

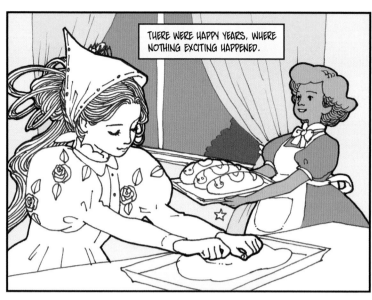

THERE WERE HAPPY YEARS, WHERE NOTHING EXCITING HAPPENED.

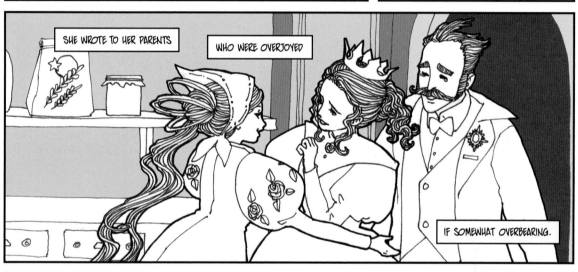

SHE WROTE TO HER PARENTS

WHO WERE OVERJOYED

IF SOMEWHAT OVERBEARING.

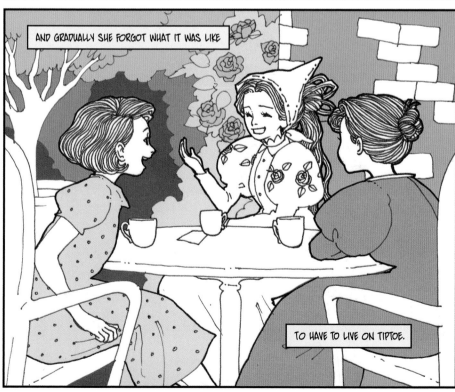

AND GRADUALLY SHE FORGOT WHAT IT WAS LIKE

TO HAVE TO LIVE ON TIPTOE.

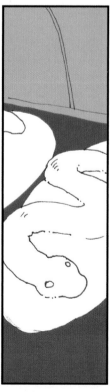

ONE AFTERNOON, AN OLD FRIEND DROPPED IN TO VISIT.

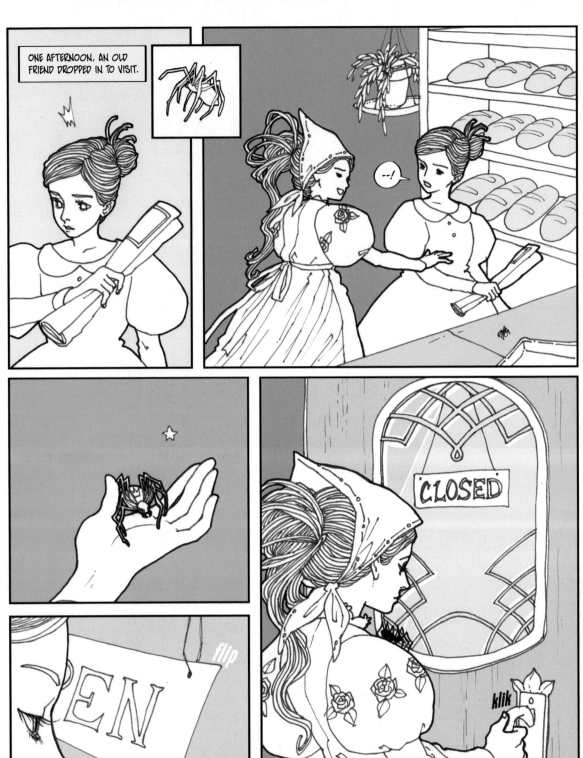

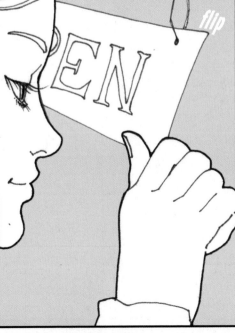

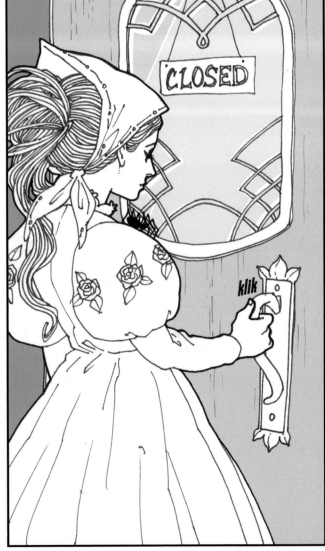

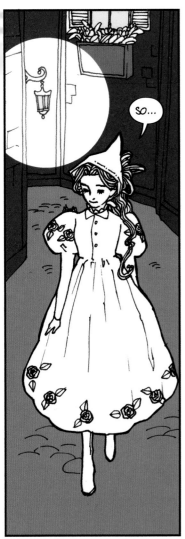

SO...

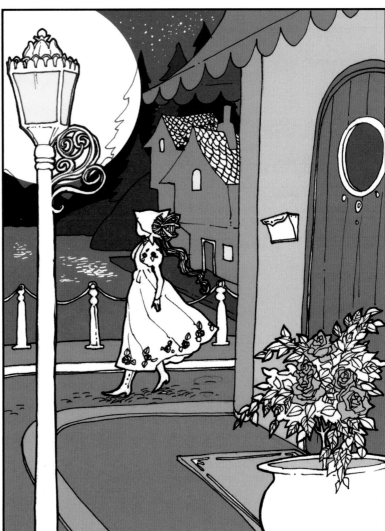

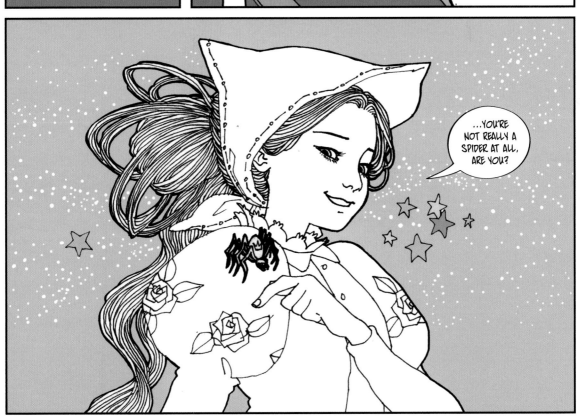

...YOU'RE NOT REALLY A SPIDER AT ALL, ARE YOU?

OH, BUT I **AM**.
A **KING** IS NO MORE THAN THE **LEAST** OF HIS PEOPLE.

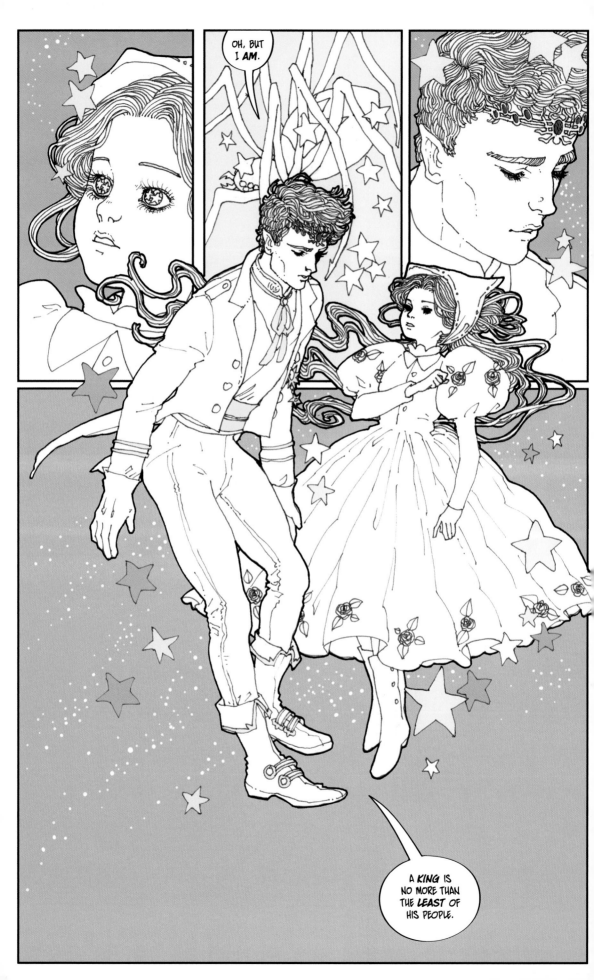

YOU LOOK WELL.
I'M SO GLAD YOU'RE ALL RIGHT.
WOULD YOU COME TO A **BALL** WITH ME?
DO I HAVE TO WEAR A STUPID DRESS?

YOU MAY WEAR WHATEVER YOU WANT.
PROMISE ME ONE THING?
WHAT?
I NEED TO BE BACK IN TIME TO OPEN THE BAKERY IN THE MORNING.
OF COURSE.
YOU HAVE MY WORD.

THIS IS MY HOME.
WOW.
IT'S... ANCHORED HERE?
ONLY TEMPOR-ARILY.
IT FLOATS ON THE BREEZE, NORMALLY.
SHALL WE?
AND SO, IN A CASTLE AT THE EDGE OF NIGHT...

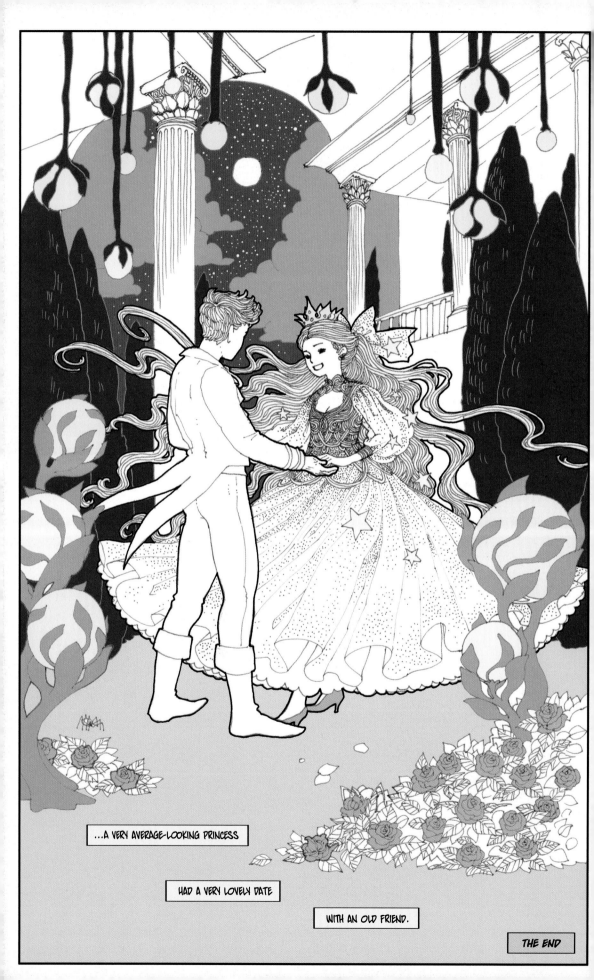

...A VERY AVERAGE-LOOKING PRINCESS

HAD A VERY LOVELY DATE

WITH AN OLD FRIEND.

THE END

Unbound

by Naomi Salman

"**A**nd there's a *sex club* downstairs," said the former tenant.

He'd spent the entire tour raving against the tiny bathroom and the narrow windows, obviously trying to get some reaction. Delio's silence seemed to put him in a mood. Maybe he had unfinished business with the owner. And well, *sure*, this place was small and dark and unfurnished; but it also meant it was affordable.

Still, Delio looked up at that last sentence. "A sex club?"

"A *sex club!*" said the guy, triumphant that his last attempt had worked. "They were careful not to tell me! I found out two days after I moved in! How could *anyone* be comfortable living upstairs from *that*?"

Delio didn't know what he should say. Especially since he was going to take the apartment anyway.

* * *

All of his worldly possessions fit in his backpack, so moving in wasn't too much of a hassle. He spent most of his first paycheck on a mattress. Then he sat on it and called Tina.

"Hey, little bro. Settling in okay?" She had a warm voice, just a little bit ironic, like she was aware at all times of some underlying cosmic joke. Delio always felt better hearing her.

"Good. Um." He looked around his apartment, but there was nothing for him to remark on. "It's good here."

"Wow, okay, don't hurt yourself. You know, I should get you one of these word-a-day calendars."

"You're not funny," he said, but he was smiling. "How's Dubai?"

"The usual. How's the place?"

"Empty. For now. I bought a mattress, though."

"Any interesting neighbors?"

"The previous tenant said there was a sex club downstairs."

He heard her choke on the line.

"A sex club? What does that look like?"

"I don't know. I didn't go and look."

"You're so fucking incurious! Here's your word of the day — *incurious*. Now go and snapchat that shit for me."

* * *

Delio didn't go looking for sex clubs. He went to work, spent the day underneath a car, checked his mailbox when he got home, then went straight for the stairs. He used his own key to open his own door. He watched the motor oil wash off him in dark curlicues under the shower, staying under the spray as long as he wanted. Then he cooked proper food, for one, and went to sleep in a bed he'd bought.

Sometimes it still felt like a dream, like he might wake up on someone else's couch with no warning.

* * *

The first time he lingered in the hall was two weeks after moving in; for some reason, his mailbox wouldn't open. He cursed at it and jiggled the key, but neither worked much.

"Hey," said a voice. "Need a hand?"

At first he thought it was a girl. Asian, with long sleek hair under a woolen hat, and delicate features. Then he took a second look. A guy, maybe. He couldn't really tell, under the green cableknit sweater. How did you ask that kind of thing?

"It's fine," Delio said belatedly. "Just stuck."

"So, not fine. Can I try?"

Delio wordlessly stepped back and watched the newcomer fiddle with his keys until the mailbox opened, prompting a smile — so wide and genuine Delio felt out of place somehow, like he'd been mistaken for someone else, a much closer friend.

"There! They all get stuck the same way."

"Thanks." He held out his hand, which went unnoticed. "I'm Delio. Morales."

"The scary new neighbor, huh? Lee Huang."

Guy, thought Delio. Then, "Scary?"

"You're big and you don't talk to anyone." Lee smiled at him, then saw his outstretched hand. "Oh — sorry."

He had long, nervous fingers, and his palm was just a bit too dry. Delio didn't want to stop talking to him just yet. He couldn't remember the last time he'd talked to a stranger out of something other than necessity.

"Thanks again," he said. "I live up in 201."

"Really? Wow, I thought it was still empty. Quietest upstairs neighbor I ever had."

"You're right underneath?"

"Sure. Why not?"

Delio cleared his throat. "The... the former tenant told me it was a sex club."

Lee kept smiling.

"Sort of, yeah. Over in the studio. 101 is just my place, though."

Delio stared, then realized he was staring. "Sorry."

The smile didn't waver. "No worries. I'll see you around."

Lee stepped outside, hunching his shoulders against the cold. Delio just stood there next to his open mailbox until he finally thought of grabbing his mail.

* * *

"So I met the..." Delio pondered his words for a moment. "The sex club guy."

Tina screamed in his ear. "Oh my God, tell me everything. Is it a huge sleazy dude?"

Delio couldn't imagine anyone further from that description than Lee. "No. He's... much smaller than me. Pretty thin. He's Asian."

"Did he proposition you? Was it super awkward?"

"No," Delio repeated with a faint twinge of annoyance.

"Oh, hey, wow. You actually liked him."

"I don't want to point and laugh, that's all."

"Pointing and laughing is fun."

"He just... he just seems like a guy, you know?"

An hour after hanging up, Delio was still thinking about what he'd told her. There was something about Lee. Obviously, he wasn't ashamed of what he did; but he hadn't tried to shock Delio, either. Probably wouldn't have brought it up at all on his own. He was just a guy. A decent guy.

* * *

The next time Delio ran into Lee, he realized he'd been waiting for it. It was like watching a movie; he was sitting back and didn't do much, but he wanted to know what happened next.

"Hey, Lee."

Lee, who was looking for his mailbox key, looked up and gave him another of his luminous smiles. "Hey." He raised his thin eyebrows. "Where have you been, man?"

Delio was still in his oil-stained clothes. "I'm a mechanic. It's a hands-on job."

"You don't say." He was wearing a tight black t-shirt this time. He really was skinny, but he had corded, veiny forearms, and his shoulders were broader than they'd looked underneath his knitted sweater.

Once again, Delio felt like talking. It was rare enough that he gave it a shot. "So... what about you? What do you do?"

Lee blinked at him.

"You know what I do," he said after a second.

"Oh. Yes." Delio hesitated. "I didn't think it was your... your *actual* job."

Lee took his mail, then slipped on his sweater. "Hey. Want to come and take a look at the studio? It's empty right now."

If it had been anyone else, Delio would have refused without thinking. But Lee had a way of making it seem reasonable. For all that he was smaller than Delio, he also radiated some kind of easy confidence. Like he always knew what he was doing. It made you want to follow him.

So Delio followed him.

They got out in the cold. Delio hadn't understood last time, but of course you couldn't have any kind of club in the tiny apartments which made up their building. The studio was right there, across the narrow alley. Lee opened the door and stepped back with a smile.

"After you."

Delio went in warily, unsure what to expect. The place was silent and still. Weak daylight streamed in from the ceiling windows, enough that he could see inside. There were straw mats on the floor and exposed beams above. Baskets in every corner, filled with soft, colored bundles.

"This doesn't look like a sex club."

Lee grinned at him, leaning against the door-frame. "It's not. We only do bondage here."

Delio realized the bundles were ropes — in every color and obviously made from different materials. It wasn't hard to imagine what the exposed beams were for. Some of them even had hooks.

"Oh."

"Yeah. The guy who lived in 201 before you — he found out and tried to sue me. I suppose he's the one who told you?"

"Yeah."

"Well, if you ever bring kids around, I promise you don't have to worry about them running into obscene behavior. My customers know we have neighbors."

Delio turned to look at him.

"I live alone," he said. "And I don't... mind. Really. I mean — it looks like a yoga class."

"It's kind of like a yoga class," Lee said, eyes

Lee did look like he could handle someone. The way Delio handled a car. Get his hands dirty, put his back into it, make it work.

twinkling. "You need comfortable clothes, and it helps to be flexible."

Delio huffed and Lee stepped back, a wordless signal that the tour was over. He locked the door behind them and they crossed the small dead-end alley again.

"Thanks for being gracious about it. I already like you better than the other guy."

You're the gracious one, Delio wanted to say, but even in his mind it didn't make a lot of sense. He looked at Lee's long fingers. It wasn't hard at all to imagine him tying up someone.

Before he went upstairs, Delio shook his hand again. Lee's grip was like he remembered, warm and dry and certain.

* * *

In the shower, Delio closed his eyes and let the warm water drown it all out.

There was something about Lee, and it wasn't the way he looked — though he was handsome, with high cheekbones, dark hair and dark eyes and golden skin, only a shade lighter than Delio's. No, it was the way he held himself. *I know what I'm doing*. The second he'd seen doubt on Delio's face, he'd just shown him the place, laid himself bare. He had nothing to hide. He was the only one who'd talked to Delio in the hall, looked him in the eye. The previous tenant had sued him, and yet he'd chosen to trust the new guy. Give him a chance. *I know what I'm doing*. He did look like he could handle someone. The way Delio handled a car. Get his hands dirty, put his back into it, make it work.

Delio took himself in hand and braced his free arm against the tiled wall, pressing his forehead in the crook of his elbow. The warm water beat at his shoulder blades. How was it to get tied up? He'd honestly never wondered. He'd always had fairly normal sex — not that he'd *had* sex in two years. Not since things had gone bad; not since they'd started to get better. He imagined himself bound, unable to move, with Lee smiling that smile at him. And it wouldn't matter. He could be trusted with it. He knew what he was doing.

"Bondage?" Tina laughed. "Man, I knew he was creepy."

Delio steered the conversation towards his job, then said he was tired and hung up.

* * *

Lee's customers came on Wednesday and Sunday nights.

Delio saw them through his blinds, a motley crowd of men and women, chatting easily, breath clouding in the cold. The studio's windows were obscured with colorful curtains; the light was on inside. Eventually, the door opened and they went in, lingering in the entrance to take off their shoes. More people trickled in during the next three hours, in pairs or alone, without knocking. From time to time, someone came out to smoke, getting it over quick because of the winter chill.

They all left around midnight, whispering and elbowing each other whenever someone laughed too loudly. They were just people, like Lee. Anything could have been going on in there.

Delio felt like he was the creepy one, watching them like that.

* * *

He didn't see Lee again for a week.

Of course, he knew where he lived, but knocking on the guy's door just didn't seem right. Delio didn't want to make things awkward, not so soon after his fresh start. It gnawed at him, though, and he made a stupid mistake at work that could've been easily avoided if he'd only paid attention.

It sent him in a cold panic, because he couldn't lose his job, he *couldn't*. He couldn't beg his sister for help again. It had been too hard pulling himself from that pit. If he slipped back in, he felt he couldn't ever climb out this time.

He ended up leaving work almost an hour late — he hadn't wanted to go, persuaded there was still something to be done, or to be *undone*, maybe, a way to erase the whole day — until his boss sighed loudly and told him to get himself home and he'd do better tomorrow.

Delio passed the studio without looking on his way home. In fact, he wasn't looking where he was going at all, didn't even turn on the light when he came into the building, and collided into Lee so brutally he almost knocked him to the ground.

"Oh — *Christ*," he said, grabbing his arm. "I'm sorry, Lee, are you—"

"It's fine, I'm fine," Lee answered, getting back his beanie. His long dark hair had spilled on his shoulders. "Delio?"

"Yeah. It's me. Sorry."

"Are you alright?"

Delio shook his head; if he answered, his voice would crack. Lee gently touched his wrist, and Delio realized he was squeezing his arm in a death grip.

"Sorry," he rasped, eyes burning as he let go. "Sorry, I'm sorry."

"I got that part." Lee was joking, but he still looked worried. He was wearing another knitted sweater, dark blue today.

There was a silence. Lee watched Delio for a moment, then cleared his throat.

"Um. Would you maybe like some tea?"

Delio felt like someone had reached inside his chest and squeezed. He thought of saying no and fleeing to his small apartment. Then he thought of being alone in the dark with his thoughts.

"If you don't mind," he managed.

"I really don't." Lee put his beanie back on. His eyes crinkled when he smiled. "C'mon."

* * *

Delio was so out of it he only realized they'd gone to the studio after Lee had gotten the lock open.

"Why — why are we here?"

"It's where I keep my stash," Lee said, taking off his shoes. "Of tea, I mean. The customers mainline it like you wouldn't believe."

The studio was just one room, but it was about five times bigger than Delio's place. It felt good, like he had more space to think. He knew, he *knew* he wasn't going to be fired — his boss had made that clear. It was just a mistake. Mistakes happened. Breathing was still hard. Delio took off his shoes, too, and stepped on the straw mat floor; it was firmer than he thought. Sitting cross-legged by a small table, he waited for Lee to bring hot water and a huge tin box filled with all sorts of tea.

"Which one?"

Delio picked at random. Lee made some for them both and poured him a cup. For a while there was nothing, just quiet, and the faint noise of Lee blowing on his tea. Delio's ears were ringing like someone had shouted at him for hours.

He waited till he'd taken a first sip to speak. "It's good. Thank you."

"Don't mention it. You looked kind of stressed out."

Lee seemed genuinely concerned about it, too. They didn't even know each other that well. Delio looked at his long graceful hands, the fine edges of his cheekbones. He was the kind of man he would have liked to draw, if he knew how.

"I was. I am. I just did something stupid at work."

"Ah, I'm sure it'll be fine."

"Yeah. I'm just..." He didn't want to explain he'd been homeless and jobless for two years, so he drank more tea. He couldn't have said what flavor it was, but it was warm.

There was a smell in the air, not bad but insistent enough he noticed it after a while. For a moment he thought it was weed. Then Lee noticed him sniffing and grinned.

"It's hemp," he said. "The ropes."

"Oh." Delio put down his cup and looked around. The lights were on, all of them hidden to bring a gentle glow to the room. Everything about this place was like Lee's sweater: soft and warm and comfortable.

They'd both taken off their shoes. There would be no quick exit like last time.

Delio felt the words bloom and burst in his mouth like a flower bud in spring. "If I wanted to try..."

"Is it okay that I've brought you here?" Lee said after a moment.

"Yeah. It's — it's fine." Delio realized he'd never smiled at Lee. When he did, tentative, Lee looked surprised — but then his answering smile went all the way to his eyes again.

"Thank you," Delio said again. "I feel better."

"It's a good place to be calm. Bondage really is a bit like yoga, you know. It's just so different from what people tend to imagine."

"Yeah?"

"Yeah. I mean... I wouldn't have created this place if I didn't love it. The people who come here, they love it too. It's just a safe place to practice." His smile had something wry in it for the first time. "Creeped out yet?"

"You've never creeped me out," Delio said, looking right at him.

He'd wanted to convey how much he meant it, but Lee held his gaze and they just looked at each other for a few silent seconds. Something passed between them, in the fragrant stillness of the wide room. Delio felt the words bloom and burst in his mouth like a flower bud in spring.

"If I wanted to try..."

His throat closed, but too late. Lee just looked at him. Without a smile on his face, his fine bones and dark eyes made him look like something otherworldly. Maybe he knew; maybe this was why he smiled so much.

"The club?" he said eventually.

"Not — not necessarily the club. I mean — I like the place, don't get me wrong. It feels — quiet. Like you said. But I'd rather..." He took a deep breath that shook around the edges. "Lee, I'm not good at this."

Lee looked at him for another second; his eyes were a bit wider than usual. He reached out, and Delio took his hand.

Lee's thumb rubbed circles in his palm. Then he laced their fingers together.

"I can tie you up," he said. "Would you like that?"

"I don't know," Delio said honestly.

"But you want to try."

"I guess so."

He couldn't have said why, but Lee didn't ask, just squeezed his fingers. "You're wearing jeans. That's not ideal."

"I can… I can take them off."

"Your shirt, too? I'll put the heating on."

"Yeah, that's — not a problem."

He expected Lee to ask about his underwear next, but he didn't. He just let go and got up to turn on the heat. While he did, Delio swallowed, then got up and stripped, without thinking too much about it. Soon enough he was only in his boxers.

"Hey," Lee said, coming back. "If something feels strange, you just speak up. Okay? I'd much rather stop in the middle than find out later you weren't into it."

"Yeah, I'll — yeah. Of course."

"Okay. Sit down. And here, catch."

Lee tossed him a bundle of rope. Delio caught it and sat down cross-legged. It was just rope, thick and brown — but he realized he'd never held any in his hands. He'd never been tied up. That stuff only really happened in the movies.

Lee put his hair up, then sat next to him and held out his hand, smiling. "You can give it back. It was just so you could get a look." He pointed at a pair of sturdy scissors hanging on the wall. "If something feels very wrong, I can always cut you free."

Delio nodded without a word.

"I want to blindfold you," Lee went on. "Is that okay?"

Delio didn't know that it was okay, but he didn't balk at the thought, either. He nodded again, cautiously. Lee got a piece of cloth from one of the baskets and went behind him to tie it over his eyes; the world went soft and dark.

What am I doing, Delio thought. He didn't even know this guy.

Then he felt Lee's hands come down along his neck to rest on his shoulders. His cool, dry hands, with long nervous fingers. Lee dug his thumbs in, wringing relief from the tense muscle; Delio leaned back and exhaled.

Lee gave *very* thorough back rubs. After some time, Delio started feeling drowsy and good, so good it bordered on painful when Lee's fingers squeezed harder. Eventually, he felt his fingers comb his hair, and then Lee kissed his neck.

"Tell me if this is going somewhere you don't like," he said again.

Delio nodded. "This I like."

"Yeah?" There was a smile in Lee's voice. He pulled Delio back against his chest, then brought his wrists in front and suddenly there was rope, bringing them together. It looped once or twice, then Lee made a knot.

Hooking up was one thing. Letting a virtual stranger restrain him was another. Delio still didn't say anything. He'd been the one to ask.

Lee made him press his wrists against his chest. The rope went over Delio's right shoulder, looped down and around his waist, then climbed up his back, coming over the left. It dug where Lee's thumbs had dug, into muscle that was already tender. It kept wrapping around his chest, over his folded arms, and Lee tightened it every once in a while, going back to check, pulling inch by inch until Delio felt utterly constrained, his wrists bound over his own heart, ropes squeezing him all over. It didn't hurt. It wasn't uncomfortable. But for all that it wasn't scary or painful, he knew it wasn't for show; already he couldn't free himself.

Somehow, he liked that thought. Struggle was a moot point, so he didn't have to fight. He could just let go.

Lee had moved away and around him to complete his harness; he knelt behind Delio again and pulled him close. His sweater was soft against Delio's bare back. He wedged one of his hands between Delio's to lace their fingers again.

> *"I can tie you up," he said. "Would you like that?"*

"How are you feeling? Any numbness?"

"I'm good," Delio said from the soft darkness he was in. Lee smelled nice. Something about his shampoo. "I... I really can't move at all."

"No, you can't." Lee squeezed his fingers. "But if you ask me to untie you, I will."

"I'm good," Delio repeated.

Lee made him lie on his back, then bent his left leg double and bound it with ropes that looped around Delio's ankle and all over his thigh. He pulled them even tighter than the ones on his chest. This was about restraining him, big and solid though he was. Lee moved on to the right leg next, and it was only when Delio was trussed up, his heart pulsing against his hands, his folded legs falling open, that he realized he was getting hard.

He was in his underwear; he couldn't hide it. With the blindfold, he couldn't even tell if Lee was looking.

"Something wrong?" Lee asked.

His hand was back around Delio's, as if to take his pulse. Delio swallowed.

"Just — sorry," he whispered.

Lee flattened his free hand over Delio's abs, close enough to his crotch that he breathed a little deeper, trying to settle his nerves.

"Is that what you're apologizing for?" His voice was smiling again, not mocking, not even teasing. "I don't mind."

"It's not..." Delio wasn't a big talker most of the time; the drowsy warmth didn't help. "It's not about that. You said."

"It could be."

Lee kissed him on the cheek again, slowly, ghosting his lips against the skin so they caught a little, running the very point of his tongue along Delio's cheekbone. No one had ever even kissed Delio on the mouth like that.

"It could be," Lee repeated. "Tell you what: I'll just wait for you to ask."

Delio heard the flat sound of a rope thrown

It was only when Delio was trussed up, his heart pulsing against his hands, his folded legs falling open, that he realized he was getting hard.

onto the straw mat, and he knew a new bundle had unrolled. Lee had him functionally bound; now he added more ropes so Delio had trouble breathing, cutting across his stomach, tightening around his waist, strapping his folded arms more tightly against his chest. He was getting lightheaded, but he kept wanting more of that feeling, of the ropes leaving their mark in his skin.

Marks were something he desperately needed. His world was so tenuously built; it felt like it could go back to nothing at any moment. Now he was tethered to himself, to this moment in the glowing studio, with Lee working him, making sure he couldn't go anywhere. At some point Lee angled Delio's head, and Delio parted his lips, wordless, to say it was okay; Lee got the message and kissed him on the mouth, slow but possessively deep.

Delio let him. He liked Lee in charge. It was what he'd wanted from day one, maybe. Lee in charge of him, with that quiet confidence, those sure hands, taking care of him — it didn't really matter how. Lee was solid to his core in a way Delio could never be, no matter how much he worked out.

He could feel Lee's long fingers at work on his chest, slipping under the ropes and tugging. Up, so Delio's torso was lifted from the ground for a few breathless seconds; sideways, so the ropes bit further into his skin. It was nearly pain but not quite, like the backrub had been. Delio gasped because this was what Lee wanted, to see what it did to him. Lee's hair must have come undone; Delio could feel it brushing his cheeks, silk-smooth, when Lee bent to kiss him again.

He heard a shuffle; Lee was taking off his sweater. Then he straddled him, and his weight took the last of Delio's breath. He exhaled deeply, relaxing into it, sinking into himself. Lee was on top of him, knees hugging Delio's sides as if to trap him completely, like he knew Delio enjoyed the feeling. He *must* know; wasn't that was this place was all about? Delio had always liked being underneath his partner, and he was growing too hot, too impatient — something about being held down, about being *handled*, about offering himself.

"Lee, please," he managed at last. "Please — now, it's *now*, I'm asking, it's too much, *please*."

Lee said nothing, just shifted his position so he was lying on Delio's side again, one hand working the ropes, tugging, shifting, twisting, and the other one reaching down, under hot fabric, fingers wrapping and then finding a rhythm. Delio took a shaky breath; the blindfold meant he couldn't use his eyes to parse out what he felt, so he just felt everything at once, like everything participated in his pleasure, and he could strain and struggle all he wanted since he was contained — no wrong moves when he couldn't move, and it was urgent now, so close, building up and up in the pit of his stomach, and he arched and strained and actually made a noise when he came, which almost never happened.

Then the edge drew back like a low tide, leaving him weak and new, breathing hard. Lee had untied the ropes constraining his stomach; the ones on his legs were coming undone now. Delio just lay there, drifting in the afterglow, secure in the knowledge he couldn't even offer to help. He was exactly where Lee wanted him.

The ropes dropped on the straw mat, slithered off his body. He felt the marks when he breathed, wondered if they would last. His mind was empty, blue skies where thoughts drifted like clouds. Lee was still close to him; whenever he had the chance, he took Delio's hand, or brushed his cheek, or squeezed his arm or his leg. Like he didn't want him to feel alone, not for one second. Delio drifted in all directions at once; the studio was expanding around him, expanding like his chest now that he could breathe, like his limbs now that he could stretch them out. He had gotten tied up for real, and now he was free again. For real.

Lee moved away for the first time, but came

He was growing too hot, too impatient – something about being held down, about being handled, about offering himself.

back quickly enough, tugging the ropes from under Delio's body so there was nothing left. Delio had made a mess on his own stomach; Lee wiped him clean, then covered him under a blanket and slipped underneath with him.

"You're shaking," he whispered.

Delio nestled in his arms again. It was a while before his breathing evened out. Eventually, Lee reached up and took off the blindfold, careful not to pull on his hair.

Delio's eyes took a long time to focus. Lee was smiling, soft and close. His dark hair was splayed on the straw mat under his head. Delio reached up, buried his fingers into it, cupping the back of his head to pull him into a kiss.

"You haven't…" He wasn't sure how to say it. He usually tried not to be a selfish lover.

"That's not why I do it. Told you — it's not a sex club." Lee's eyes, crinkling at the corners, always smiling. "Are you alright?"

"Yeah. I feel… I don't know. That went deep." Delio exhaled. "It was really nothing like I expected."

"Try something new every day." His thumb followed Delio's mouth. "You put a lot of trust in me there."

Delio closed his eyes. "You telling me that was dumb?"

"Could've been. But then, you're a big guy. I could've been in trouble too."

"No." Delio opened his eyes again. "You know what you're doing."

Lee's thumb rubbed gently at his cheekbone. "Seems like you also do."

And it was true, Delio realized. He had a place to live, and a job he wasn't going to lose so easily. He had a neighbor who might just like him back. It was all new and tentative. But it was here to stay. He could do this; he knew how. He was doing it already.

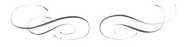

It's the Queen's reincarnation!
Kill her!
Legacies
By Sarah Winifred Searle
Here's your opening!

slmp
How do you feel?
Good work tonight, Poppy. Let's go home.
I... I'll be fine. Thank you, both.

Wisteria University
12 new text messages, 5 missed calls, 3 voice mails
16:42
Ivy: Do you need to talk? Can I bring you some food, maybe?
Sage: We're worried about you. It's been days.
Mom: I know you're busy with work, but we miss you. Dad's hoping you can visit this yea
What should I tell him?

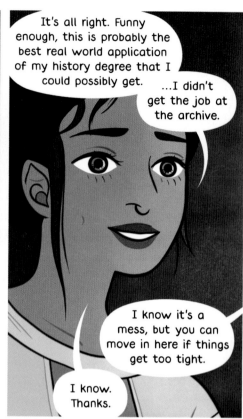

It's all right. Funny enough, this is probably the best real world application of my history degree that I could possibly get.

...I didn't get the job at the archive.

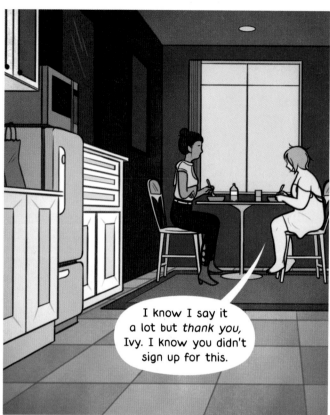

I know I say it a lot but *thank you*, Ivy. I know you didn't sign up for this.

I know it's a mess, but you can move in here if things get too tight.

I know. Thanks.

And what about *you?* You were so passionate about your studies when we met, but you haven't mentioned them in ages. I miss your rants about imperialism.

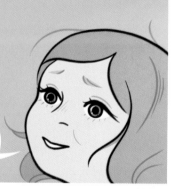

Heh, yeah. It's hard to get revved up when it turns out your past self was *complicit* in everything you've *worked against*.

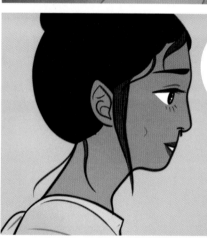

Oof. But you know, maybe that puts you in a unique position to create *change* in the world.

Hmm...

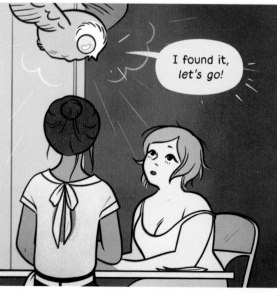

I found it, *let's go!*

The closer you feel to your old self, Poppy, the easier your ascension will be. We're looking for any relics that could illuminate *memories* of your *past lives.*
Hidden doors were common in the era when this level was built.
Over time, any gaps in the wood paneling should have grown more obvious...
Please take care. We have magic to keep us safe, but you're—
—Just a plain ol', un-special human being. I know, I know.
But *look!*

Did you find something?
I... I didn't *realize.* Poppy—
Destiny!
No.
I'm sorry, Sage. I care for you so deeply, but never in that way.

The fate of Freyfar *depends on us,* Poppy. On *you,* and your legacy as Queen. If we stray from the designated path—
How could I possibly forget?
I've only given up everything that's ever been important to me for this duty. My family, my ambitions, all *lost.*
But this? This is *mine.*
Perhaps love and marriage are *separate* for people in our position. Perhaps it's just a human hinderance until you've ascended to your throne.
I don't want to lose my *humanity,* too!
Come on, Sage. What do *you* want? And I mean *you* you, not the knight that's hitched a ride on your soul.
I can't bear the responsibility for that risk! ***I can't ask Freyfar to pay the price for my own selfishness!***

Neither of us asked for this life but we accepted it anyway. We've given it *everything.* But listen—
The world is changing, and so have we. We're not the people we once were, and maybe *that* will be this kingdom's saving grace in the end.
You'll always be my partner, Sage.
But I've found someone who gives me a reason to live for *myself,* and who challenges and inspires me to become the kind of person who truly *deserves* to lead.
And *you* deserve the chance for that happiness, too.
We three will create a better world *together.*
Thank you.

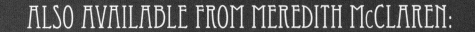
HINGES
BOOK 3 : MECHANICAL MEN

MEREDITH MCCLAREN

"From the first page to the last, I was invested...
McClaren's story feels like the the best parts of a silent
film, Disney animated short and a Hayao Miyazaki film."
— Agents of Geek

MAYDAY

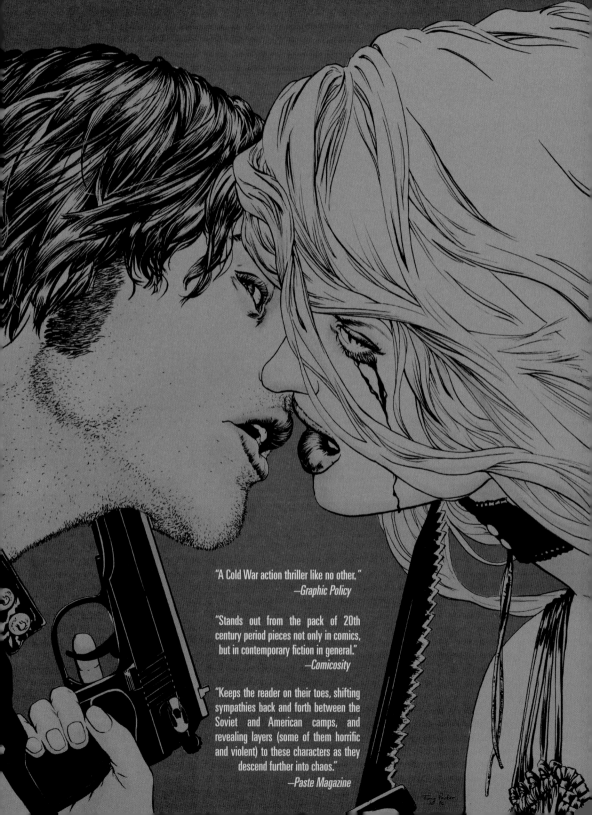

"A Cold War action thriller like no other."
—*Graphic Policy*

"Stands out from the pack of 20th century period pieces not only in comics, but in contemporary fiction in general."
—*Comicosity*

"Keeps the reader on their toes, shifting sympathies back and forth between the Soviet and American camps, and revealing layers (some of them horrific and violent) to these characters as they descend further into chaos."
—*Paste Magazine*

Also available from Alex de Campi, Carla Speed McNeil & Jenn Manley Lee:
NO MERCY
"Alex de Campi's scarily believable premise combines with Carla Speed McNeil's unbelievably beautiful art for a thriller with its brake line cut." - Brian K. Vaughan
DRAGOTTA

GORO

YAMAHA

Also by Margaret Trauth:

When the fastest woman ever built is dragged outside of reality by her ex-boyfriend, she's got to pull herself together across four parallel worlds before a hive-mind can take over the planet.

That is, assuming it hasn't already.

egypt.urnash.com/rita

"That rarest and most refreshing of things: a science-fiction story that feels like it comes from the future."
— Phil Foglio *(Girl Genius)*

"This is pure glossy adrenaline... It's utterly fantastic work."
— Steve Morris *(Comics Alliance)*

"Deliriously confusing and addictive... It's kind of wonderful."
— Peter Watts *(Blindsight)*

"Seriously folks, if you haven't looked at Decrypting Rita yet you really ought to. Very post-singularity, much upload, wow."
— Charlie Stross *(Accelerando)*

available on comixology for a few bucks, as a three-foot wide book with spot gloss interiors for a few more, or free online!

THE TAROT OF THE SILICON DAWN

A thoroughly modern Tarot deck: a gleeful, femmy hybrid of the Thoth and Golden Dawn decks that refuses to be taken entirely seriously, and is fully capable of giving you the finger.

99 cards. Some with hidden images that only appear when the light is just right.

Comes with a full-color book that will tell you *some* of its secrets.

egypt.urnash.com/tarot

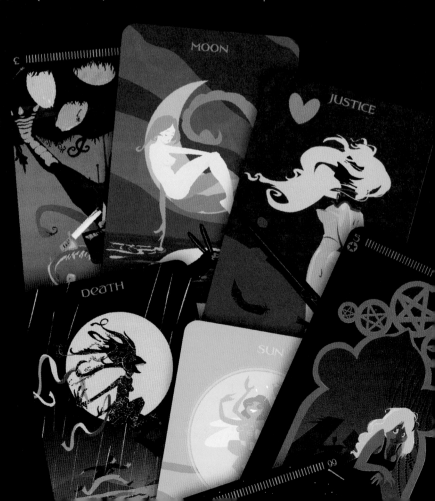

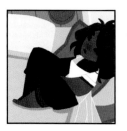

Meredith McClaren

Writer/Artist, *Would You Even Know It?* Meredith does comics. You may have heard of some (*HINGES, Hopeless Savages v4, Heart in a Box*). She lives in a constant state of exhaustion. Approach with caution. She is on tumblr, storenvy and patreon as meredithmcclaren, and twitter as @iniquitousfish.

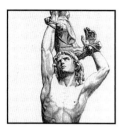

Naomi Salman

Writer, *Unbound*. Naomi was definitely not replaced by a poorly disguised clone of herself sometime in the past two years. She lives in the area of Paris that Must Not Be Named due to a bitter defeat against Julius Caesar. She is addicted to English punctuation, which is far superior to the French antiquated system. She has four potted plants on her bookshelves and a giant sword on her mantelpiece. tumblr/twitter: @naomisalman.

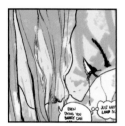

Sarah Horrocks

Writer/Artist, *Red Medusa*. Sarah is a comics creator and critic residing in Oklahoma with two large dogs. She has done cover work for Image Comics and Boom!, and self-published *The Leopard, Leviathan, Hecate* and other comics. Her ongoing comic *Goro* has just published its sixth issue and is available at mercurialblonde.storenvy.com. She is on twitter, tumblr and patreon as @mercurialblonde.

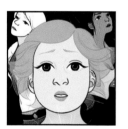

Sarah Winifred Searle

Writer/Artist, *Legacies*. Sarah Winifred Searle originally hails from spooky New England but currently lives in sunny Perth, Australia, which confuses her gothic nature. She writes and draws comics inspired by intimacy of all sorts, history, and the need for better diversity in media. Keep up with her work on social media (@swinsea) and on her website (swinsea.com)!

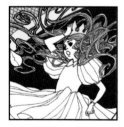

Trungles

Artist, *Treasured*. Trungles (Trung Le Nguyen) is a comic book artist and illustrator working out of Minnesota. He has contributed work for Oni Press, Boom! Studios, Limerence Press, and Image Comics. He is particularly fond of fairy tales, kids' cartoons, and rom-coms of all stripes. He is @trungles on twitter and instagram (and trungles.com) but the best place to follow his comics is patreon.com/trungles!

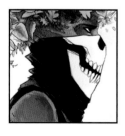

Vita Ayala

Writer, *Back At Your Door*. Vita is a queer Afro-Latinx writer out of New York City, where they live with their wife and cat sons. They have written for DC, Dark Horse, Image, and Valiant Comics, as well as having creator-owned work through Black Mask Studios (*The Wilds*) and Vault Comics (*Submerged*). They're non-stop, like Hamilton! They're available for your twitter delectation and admiration at @definitelyvita.

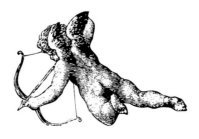

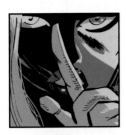

Alex de Campi

Anthology editor; writer of *Old Flames, Twinkle & The Star, Invincible Heart,* and *Treasured*. Alex has written the critically acclaimed Image miniseries *NO MERCY, MAYDAY* and *VALENTINE* as well as many, many more comics. Her most recent book has been the Havana mob noir *Bad Girls* (Gallery 13/Simon & Schuster). She believes in HEAs and may be found on instagram, twitter, tumblr and patreon as @alexdecampi.

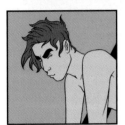

Alejandra Gutiérrez

Artist, *Twinkle & The Star*. Alejandra lives in Portland, OR and can be found on twitter as @effalope and tumblr & instagram as @hellewoods.

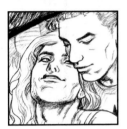

Carla Speed McNeil

Artist, *Invincible Heart*. Carla thought herself a widow at sixteen when her BFF turned out not to be the love of her life. Luckily, there were plenty more odd fish in the barrel. She bonded with her best one in a janky bar over a signed & numbered Moebius/Jodorowsky album after karate practice. Read: *Finder* (Dark Horse) and *NO MERCY*. She is @cspeedmcneil on twitter, @jargogle on tumblr and carlaspeedmcneil on patreon.

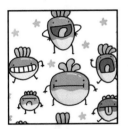

Jess Bradley

Writer, *The Last Minute*. Jess is a comic book artist and writer from the UK. As well as working for *The Phoenix Comic* and *The Beano*, she self-publishes her own comics. She spends a lot of her time trying to get her two-year-old into Synthwave. Her website is jessbradley.com and her internets are @venkmanproject on twitter and @squid-bits on tumblr.

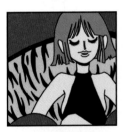

Katie Skelly

Artist, *Old Flames*. Katie is a Brooklyn-based comics creator in love with 1970s trash cinema. Her latest release is *The Agency*, a collection of erotic comics, which follows up her breakthrough hit *My Pretty Vampire* (both, Fantagraphics). She also recently completed her Bad Girl Tarot. Her website is katieskellycomics.com and she is @nurse_nurse on twitter and @skellyskellyskelly on instagram.

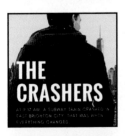

Magen Cubed

Writer, *Leather & Lace*. Magen is a novelist, occasional critic, lazy academic, known Fannibal, and your local goth girlfriend. Her stories about monsters and the people that love them (as Magen Cubed) and her erotica (as Morgan May) are available on Amazon. Magen lives in Florida with her girlfriend Melissa and a little dog named Cecil. She is @magencubed on most social media.

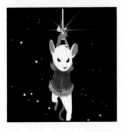

Margaret Trauth

Writer/Artist, *Olivia Lies, Pierced*. Margaret grew up in New Orleans. After a few years in the Hollywood animation scene and a gender transition, she ended up in Seattle, where she's presently busy drawing further adventures of Olivia and the Baron, and posting them at http://egypt.urnash.com/parallax/. She is on twitter and tumblr as @egypturnash.